UNDERSTANDING TOWNS

For most of us, towns are just a meaningless mass of
bricks and concrete, glass and tarmac; but observed
carefully and in detail our urban environment can become
a fascinating social study. By detecting and recognizing
the signs which you will find all around you – from
the types of building bricks used and "ordinary" house
design, to road systems and the location of rail and other
transport terminals – you can build up a picture of the
fortunes, functions and character of your town.

Understanding Towns is a study of the major factors
which determine the shape and design of towns – transport,
the demand for land, population changes, planning,
town centres and suburban housing. With each chapter
there is a special study section on one important aspect
of the general topic covered. With the chapter on
transport for example we learn how roads have developed
and how road surfaces, signs and patterns have changed.
To complete the book there is an in-depth study of one
particular town – Runcorn – which illustrates all the
processes involved in town growth and change.

WAYLAND PUBLISHERS

UNDERSTANDING TOWNS

David Stenhouse

Below: Fig. 2 **Styles in the Central Area. The four buildings shown here illustrate many of the architectural changes which have taken place in the last century. The one on the extreme left is neo-Classical of high quality. Left centre is neo-Gothic of the Railway Age. Right centre is twentieth-century "Odeon Cinema" style, and on the right is a modernistic shopping precinct.** *Left: Fig. 1* **Still a common sight in many towns — houses in decay.**

To Geoffrey

Acknowledgements
The author and publishers thank all those who have helped in the preparation of this book.
For technical advice:
    Officers of Liverpool City Council, especially the City Planning Officer, the City Building Surveyor and the City Engineer.
    The Chief Fire Officer, Merseyside County Council.
For information and assistance:
    Runcorn Development Corporation.
    The Pilkington Glass Museum, St Helens.
    Frank McGonigall, for his help with the photographs.
For illustrations used in this book on the pages indicated:
Aerofilms Limited, 8, 11, 26 bottom, 69
Professor Arthur Ling (Runcorn New Town Master Plan), 111 top, 113 top left, 113 bottom
Manchester Evening News, 62
North Western Museum of Science and Technology, 67 top
Pilkington Brothers Limited, 38 (spinning crown glass)
Runcorn Development Corporation, 112 bottom, 113 top right, 114, 115
Shelter, frontispiece, 91

SBN 85340 440 2
Copyright © 1977 by David Stenhouse
First published by Wayland (Publishers) Limited
49, Lansdowne Place, Hove, East Sussex BN3 1HS
Printed in Great Britain by
The Camelot Press Ltd, Southampton

Contents

List of Tables

1 Introduction

Most British people live in towns and cities; the urbanization of land and people has been a feature in this country more than in almost any other. This book is about urban areas and their characteristics. Most of the characteristics referred to are visible ones. They can be found and studied by any careful observer in most British towns. The term "urban landscape" refers to all the components which go to make up the total urban unit. Each town, or city, displays a variety of buildings and streets, decorated with signs and other "street furniture". The buildings vary in height, depth and style; the streets in terms of width and surface. These details have grown and changed, as the whole urban area itself has developed. Each stage in the area's development will have left behind certain features in the built environment. It is possible to look at towns and cities almost as living creatures, which respond to change by adapting their characteristics.

Most large urban areas have books written on their architecture, but their authors have concentrated, in the main, on the large public buildings, and on the churches and mansions. There are also books which deal with the development of individual features, such as houses, or parks and gardens. But even these tend to deal with the exceptional, such as the medieval timber-framed house. However, the greatest part of the area of every British town or city is made up of buildings which will never win a place in architectural textbooks. They are not in themselves individual or interesting structures; to most people the common features of the built-up area which they see around them are dull and nondescript, similar to those in many other towns. But look closely at them and the differences can be seen, the clues to your town's history and development. Each of the variations, in size, or in design, or in material, is due to some human factor, past or present.

By examining, in detail, the features and evolution of buildings, streets and the rest of the urban landscape, we will be better able to understand how our environment has formed into its present arrangement. We need to understand it, because for so many of us the urban landscape is the one we see for fifty weeks of the year. Because we have it around us all the time, we tend not to look too closely at it. But it is quite as interesting as the rural landscape, which is attractive often largely through unfamiliarity. Every day, town dwellers pass through the diversity of their own landscape, and even though some people notice some of the features, few understand their significance. This book introduces a number of themes which may help this understanding. Included are economic approaches, land-use studies, building technology, social factors, transport themes and planning.

Basic to the understanding of the urban landscape is the necessity for observation. Unless one looks closely it is possible to miss many of the characteristics which give the clues. There is so much to see, and you will not be able to find a rational explanation for all of it. For example, some features, such as size, or geographical concentration, may be understood in terms of the economics of land use. But others, such as the beauty or decorative peculiarity of a building, or again, sheer size, may have to be put down to the eccentricity of the builder. But in spite of the enormous variation possible in our towns and cities, we shall see that there are underlying uniformities, which make it possible to look for reasoned explanations for many of the features they have in common. Most of the illustrations in this book are un-named, with no place of reference, and this is intentional. The aim is not to seek the exceptional, but, instead, to look for similarities. It should be possible for readers to see their own town, or city, in the photographs and illustrations. If urban areas do have wide bands of similarity, then it is because common factors operate within and between them. It is with these factors that this book is primarily concerned. Until recently, geographical writings on towns have tended to concentrate on general, descriptive features. Most people are aware of terms such as "route centre", or "gap town", used to describe what were supposed to be underlying reasons for the growth of particular urban areas. Many of these were associated with factors of site or situation. Superimposed on these guides to growth, were the presence, or absence, of important minerals such as coal or iron, and the excellence of the communication. By adding together all the positive features a particular location had, it was possible to explain whether it had grown, or stagnated. This approach to urban studies had major pitfalls. Generally the explanations were applied to towns which were already fully developed, where the processes had perhaps taken place centuries before. It was often very difficult to find strong evidence for the importance of particular factors, so that judgement tended to be subjective. Also, the relative influence of the various themes was very difficult to define; how crucial had been a feature such as the presence of a gap through hills as compared to other factors? In reality, the growth of any town is an enormously complex business, with a great many causes of expansion, all linked together and not easily studied in isolation. To attempt to classify towns according to the predominance of one factor was a gross over-simplification.

Over the last fifty years there have been many rapidly-developing areas of the world where urban growth could be observed and, when studies were made in these areas, the whole style of urban geography changed, away from describing sites and situations and towards examinations which attempt to explain growth by means of more precise and trustworthy material. Many of the approaches have come from the USA where the features of town growth and development were to be seen in action, and compressed into a short period of time. As their towns and cities expanded, the Americans were able to see more clearly how particular characteristics developed. Of special relevance to the material in this book, they observed processes which tended to sort the whole area into zones. Offices and shops tended to cluster together, developing a physical concentration which drove out other uses of land space, especially housing. Houses too seemed to be sorted into zones, with the rich, being able to finance the high cost of commuting, living at some distance from their work; the poor, on the other hand, remained close to their factories.

From the study of these arrangements, came ideas on social and functional patterns in towns and cities. Theoretical "models" were provided which tried to show what could happen as towns expanded. Figure 3 shows the most commonly used of these models, fifty years old now, but included in most recent books on towns. This concentric approach has been used to show how functional

and social zoning might take place. These new approaches also looked at the location of particular functions in the urban area. For example, it is possible to map the distribution of solicitors, or cinemas, or churches within the town. The patterns which emerge might be explained by comparing them with access to transport facilities, or population density. Increasingly, many of the conclusions of these studies are shown in mathematical terms, the language of the modern social scientist.

There is, then, a tendency to look at urban areas as economic creations, with internal differences due to socio-economic factors, arranged in geometrical patterns and having characteristics which can be compressed into mathematical symbols. This type of approach has been a great improvement on the older, comparatively unscientific one. At least it means that conclusions are based on real information. But although such an approach is invaluable when dealing with the total urban area, much of the human element in the urban landscape is lost or hidden. We must, however, include reference to this type of study, and chapter two is concerned with the land-economics approach to town features. After that we will return to a more human and personal view of the landscape and its explanation.

At the end of each of the chapters is a list of materials for reference and suggestions for further study. The books are arranged so that generally the first-named is the least complex, at least where there are more than a couple of entries. There are also many other sources of information, which involve personal research but which can yield very interesting results, which may not be available without this individual effort. In some of the chapters there are ideas for fieldwork, although this is not a book concerned primarily with method, and there are references to reliable textbooks on techniques.

Below: Figs. 3 and 4 **Land use models. The concentric model (left) is the simplest, and is the work of E. W. Burgess, an American sociologist. He outlined the model in 1925, after studies in Chicago. It might be taken as the probable arrangement in rapidly-growing industrial cities. Burgess's zonal analysis of Chicago is shown below right.**

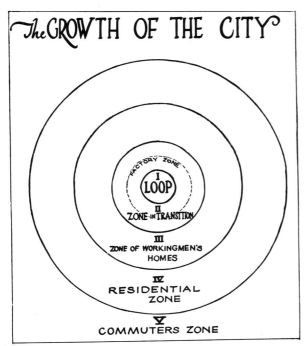

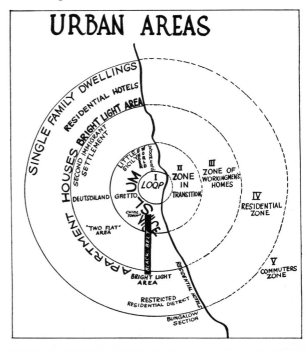

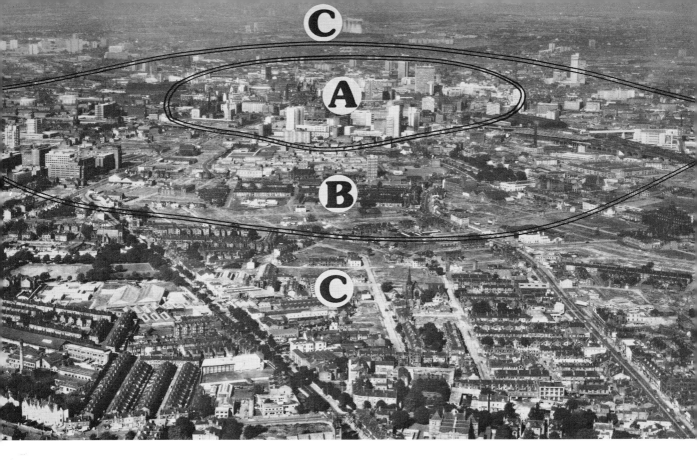

Above: Fig. 5 **Concentric zones in Manchester and,** *below, Fig. 6,* **in Leeds.**

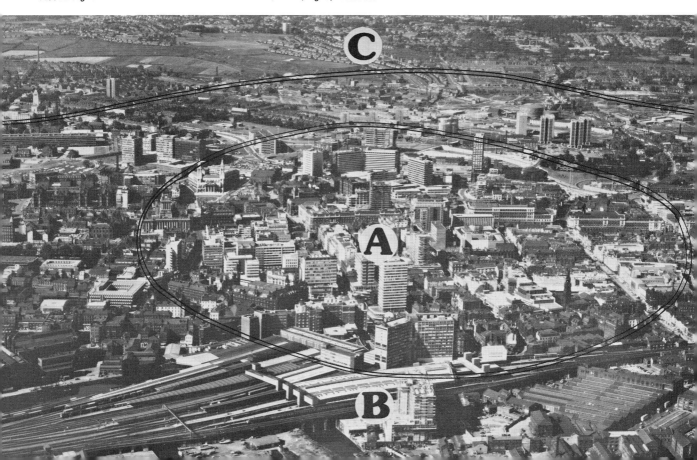

2 Land economics and zonation

Anyone who moves about a town, or better still, a large city, must be aware of the differences between the various sections. Most large urban areas have a recognizable centre, where there is a concentration of retail and commercial business in the form of shops and offices. To most people it is obvious that the outer fringes of the area, the suburban zones, are taken up mainly by residential property, although, on the extreme perimeter, there may be significant sections of modern, space-seeking industry. Other parts have no single clear characteristic, containing fragments of housing, industry and commerce. But, generally there are discernible patterns within the urban area, with each zone having its own identity, with a broad similarity of function for the buildings within it.

The pattern of zonation is usually quite distinct as can be seen from aerial photographs of most large British cities. Figures 5 and 6 show Leeds and Manchester and it is possible to see a similarity in their arrangement, although the scale of development is different. The centres (A) can be distinguished physically because of the concentration of high-rise building. Within this Central Area is an accumulation of specialized services, such as solicitors, accountants, furniture and electrical shops, dealing with the total needs of the urban unit. Around it is a mixed area (B) containing transport facilities, small factories, warehouses and some poorer-quality housing. Beyond this, the mainly residential zones (C) extend to the limits of the area, although there is a wide variety in the individual housing types. On the horizon are the more recent suburban estates, together with the more modern industrial development.

The fundamental factor behind this patterning is the demand for land and the price people can afford to pay for it. In the medieval period, when towns were small, their influence did not extend very far, mainly because of poor transport facilities. Each street contained a variety of houses and businesses. Obviously, there would always be more desirable areas, such as the market square for business, or the urban fringe for the houses of the rich, but because the internal area of the average town was small, people were able to reach all parts easily. Therefore there were no really prime locations in terms of accessibility. In the last hundred and fifty years, with improvements in transport, towns have rapidly expanded. Often, the roads and railways met or terminated near the centre. The road pattern of most towns was developed before the area grew and already focussed on the centre. In the nineteenth century, when the railways were built, passengers wanted to travel as near to the centre

as possible, and many of the stations were built on the fringes of the Victorian town centres. Better transport facilities made it easier for people to reach the centre than any other part of the town or city. This accessibility made the zone a place of great attraction. The factory owner felt that he could assemble his materials very cheaply, because of low transport costs; the office worker could see that he could save himself much time in travelling to work. Some people considered it not just desirable but essential for them to be within the central zone. Specialized shopping, business and professional services needed to tap the whole population of the urban area, if they were to prosper. If we look at the trade of barristers or goldsmiths, we see that they need to draw their customers from a wide area because only a small fraction of the total population needs them at any one time. The goods and services they provide are expensive and we do not use them frequently. We could contrast them with the "corner-shop" grocer, found in almost all areas of the town but seldom in the centre. Their trade is in goods we use all the time and would not travel large distances for.

When many functions are competing for the occupation of a small area, one which is too small to accommodate all the demands, then the result is a rapid rise in the value of the land, or the rent which will be paid for it. In this way those who feel that they really need the land will get it by paying most for it. Some potential users very quickly find that they cannot afford the price asked. The amount each group is prepared to pay, called the bid rent, varies according to how essential they consider a central location to be. The diagram in Figure 7 attempts to show how various land users react to the advantage of central location by varying their bid rent. This is an idealized arrangement, which

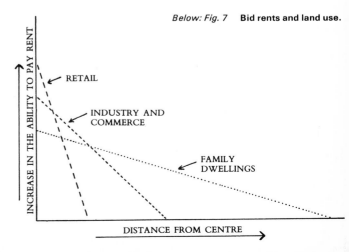

Below: Fig. 7   **Bid rents and land use.**

INCREASE IN THE ABILITY TO PAY RENT

← RETAIL

← INDUSTRY AND COMMERCE

← FAMILY DWELLINGS

DISTANCE FROM CENTRE

attempts to show how user groups would behave if there were no factors other than financial. Now, of course, we have all sorts of controls in operation, particularly those applied by governments. In most societies there is no longer a situation where financial power is the sole criterion of development. Retail users will pay a high central rent, but their rate of decrease as sites are located further and further out from the centre is less than that of retailing because they can still function efficiently in less-accessible areas. In the case of people wishing to develop land for residential use, they are prepared to pay little more for central positions than perimeter ones. In the competition for central space, they rapidly capitulate and there are few towns where housing appears, to any great extent, within the centre.

When the use of land is determined by financial power, then each zone is won by the highest bidder. The result of this is the pattern shown previously in the aerial photographs. These arrangements are often shown in diagrammatic form, where the successive zones appear as concentric circles, sectors or, in a fragmented pattern, according to the local conditions which are considered to operate. The three most widely-used theoretical forms are shown in Figures 3, 8, 9. The concentric one has been referred to previously, but we can look at it again because, if Figures 5 and 6 are translated into two-dimensional diagrams, they emerge as concentric arrangements. The diagrams will not be used in this book, although the distributions they suggest will be referred to.

The importance of the land-economics approach is that it broadly explains the sorting processes which produce "normal" patterns. It must be understood that the zonation which results is not an accidental feature; there is a degree of inevitability about it. In small urban units, shops, offices, houses and factories may still be jumbled together. In large towns and cities the functions begin to separate and, as we have seen, the offices and specialist shops tend to cluster in the centre while other sections have their own concentrations, as in industrial estates. The greatest degrees of specialization and separation should therefore be found in the largest conurbations.

Towards the edges of the urban areas, demand for land may be less. One reason for this is that, unless there are restrictions on the growth of the town, the boundaries can be expanded, capturing new land and satisfying all demands. By contrast, the Central Area cannot be expanded to any great extent. The reason for the competition for land has been its maximum accessibility within the urban unit. A movement, even a short distance from the centre, brings a rapid decline in this accessibility. Because of this, the edge of the Central Area is often a very pronounced boundary, and outside the zone of prestige offices and shops, the land use changes rapidly. It is possible to find, behind the glossy frontages of main street shopping, old-established, family businesses still in their original buildings. With them are other functions absent from the competitive centre, such as old warehouses, small wholesalers and derelict open spaces.

Figs. 8 and 9   **Land use models. In 1939, Homer Hoyt, after studying rent patterns in twenty-five US cities, put forward what has been called the sectorial theory. He was mainly concerned with residential use, and especially with high-quality housing. We might use this approach in studying how frequently the highest quality housing in Britain lies in the south-western parts of towns and cities, because westerly winds were supposed to** carry smoke and smells away from them. In 1945, Chauncy Harris and E. L. Ullman introduced a multiple nuclei model. Very few British urban areas are arranged in this way, because our centres tend to have strong attractive influences. It is possible to combine the models, for example the concentric and sectorial, so as to give more complex arrangements.

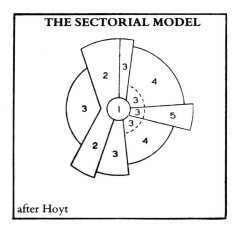

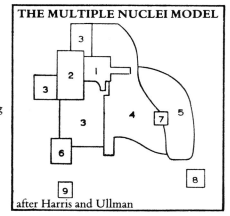

1 Central business district
2 Wholesale light manufacturing
3 Low-class residential
4 Medium-class residential
5 High-class residential
6 Heavy manufacturing
7 Outlying business district
8 Residential suburb
9 Industrial suburb

Above: Fig. 10   **Tower blocks in Croydon's Central Area.**

Central Areas are perhaps less important now than they were before the rapid rise in car ownership which has made the fixed lines of transport, such as bus routes and railway lines, less important. However, even now, demand for space in the centre is greater than for any other area. If the Central Area cannot expand horizontally, it must do so vertically. Our present, high-rise centres, concentrations of tower blocks, shown dramatically in the photograph of Croydon (Figure 10) are the results of competition for space. They represent the peak of demand, and of intensity of use, within urban areas.

Guide to further study

Bibliography
General books on urban geography, which include greater detail on urban zones, are

A. E. Smailes, *The Geography of Towns* (Hutchinson, 1966)
J. H. Johnson, *Urban Geography. An introductory analysis* (Pergamon, 1972)
E. Jones, *Towns and Cities* (Oxford University Press, 1966)
H. Carter, *The Study of Urban Geography* (Arnold, 1972)

Interesting studies can be made of the distribution of individual trades and professions. Details of their location can be found in

(a) The Yellow Pages classified directory published by the Post Office.
(b) The Classified Trades sections of local directories. The most familiar ones are those published by Kelly. They give lists of the names and addresses of specialized groups and also information on residential matters. Early editions of any local directory are particularly interesting because they often give the occupations of the householder and can be used for studies of the social character of an area. Local directories generally date from the mid-eighteenth century. Usually this information dies out soon after the beginning of this century.

These sources provide the information which can be plotted to produce a pattern. For analysis of these patterns see the "method" books listed at the end of chapter eleven.

One book which combines the theoretical background to urban features with suggestions on methods of handling data is

J. A. Everson and B. P. Fitzgerald, *Inside the City* (Longman, 1972). This is referred to in more detail in the appendix to chapter eleven.

3 History

– from multi-purpose to single-purpose buildings and areas

The previous chapter dealt with the contrasts between the different functional zones of the modern city, or large town. This development has been of relatively recent origin in British towns and cities, with the exception of London. It has become a feature almost entirely within the last two hundred years. The medieval city was compact, its size related to the distance one could travel by the main forms of transport: walking and horse-drawn traffic. Most towns were small in terms of population. In the fourteenth century, London had a population of around 23,000, far outstripping all others, few of which had more than four or five thousand inhabitants. There was little in the way of land-use patterning in these towns. One main factor in this was that, until the nineteenth century, most houses were also places of work, with the ground-floor rooms acting as shops, workshops, stables and slaughterhouses. The following extracts give some idea of the character of the medieval merchant house.

"But compared to modern life, the medieval urban family was no private unit: it included, as part of the normal household, not only relatives by blood but a group of industrial workers as well as domestics whose relationship was that of secondary members of the family.

"The workshop was a family: likewise the merchant's counting house. The members ate together at the same table, worked in the same room, slept in the same dormitory, joined in the family prayers, participated in the common amusements.

"The fact that the burgher house served as workshop, store and counting house prevented any zoning between these functions. The competition for space between the domestic and the working quarters, as business grew and the scale of production expanded, was also perhaps responsible for encroachment over the original back gardens by sheds, storage bins and special workshops. Mass production and the concentration of looms in great sheds was known in Flanders in the fourteenth century, and operations like fulling, milling, glassmaking, and iron-making required a more isolated type of workshop: in these industries came the earliest break between living and working."

From Lewis Mumford, *The Culture of Cities*, 1938, pp. 35, 39–40.

Dairymen, cow-keepers and other small farmers often lived in the town, keeping some of their stock in their houses, and taking them through the streets on their way to graze. As late as 1840, thousands of sheep and cattle were driven through the streets of the City of London, destined for the Smithfield Meat Market. The larger towns might have a concentration of merchants and retailers in one place, London being the best example, but, in most of them, the sorting processes were poorly developed. If the population grew, the urban areas seldom extended themselves very far. The normal response was to increase the density of population, either by cramming more buildings into the same area, or by increasing the height of the buildings. Whichever method was chosen resulted in a continued mixture of all the functions of the town. Transport facilities were, as yet, too few and too slow to attract many town workers towards the countryside.

There was some segregation of groups and functions. From the eleventh century onwards, small numbers of merchants moved their houses away from the towns, and some skilled tradesmen followed them. The advantages in this movement lay in paying lower taxes, in lower food prices and in escaping from the restrictions of the craft guilds. Some groups lived apart for reasons concerned with their ethnic background. The Jews were the best example of people often separated from the main body of the town; later, the Huguenots from France showed the same isolation.

The eighteenth and nineteenth centuries saw the great explosion of urban areas, because of an increased rate of technical and economic development and a higher level of population growth. The expansion of population began the process of sorting which produced our present zonation patterns. People became more mobile and the rich seized the opportunity to escape from towns which, because of overcrowding, were becoming very unhealthy. London, once more, was the outstanding example of the process. It became fashionable to live in the country, but there were only small sections of the population which could enjoy the

sensation. The following passage refers to the growth of the West End of London:

"In 1801 the recent increase of houses is ascribed to a change of manners according to which merchants 'make a part of their well-being consist in living in a different quarter of the town from that in which they work'. The custom caused much surprise among foreign observers, and it was remarked that it was one only possible to the English with their passion for exercise in the open air. It was long before the practice was extended to the poorer section of the community."

From Dorothy George, *London Life in the Eighteenth Century*, 1925. Passage taken from the Peregrine edition, 1966, p. 104.

Literature began to make rural life attractive, with romantic ideas on the value and dignity of communicating with Nature. By the middle of the nineteenth century the country estate was the middle-class aim, a life of genteel tea parties, with the greatest excitement being the arrival of a new vicar. Popular accounts of life in towns moved away from the attractions of the Court and clubs towards views dominated by Gin Palaces and the underworld of the organized pickpockets and professional beggars. As the country, or, failing that, the suburbs, became the only "respectable" place to live, so the towns expanded. The process, which was begun by the rich, was carried on by a growing middle class. First doctors and lawyers moved out, followed by others lower in the social scale, through and down to the clerks, foremen and eventually the manual worker. The greatest single cause of this relocation of housing from the centre was the provision of cheaper transport. One important event affecting the larger areas was the Cheap Trains Act of 1883, which forced railway companies to run workmen's trains at specified times. In the case of London, by 1912, these cheap workmen's tickets represented forty per cent of all journeys within 12 kilometres ($7\frac{1}{2}$ miles) of the centre.

The ability to move depended on purchasing power. The poor had little in the way of disposable income. Their wages were low and there was nothing left for luxuries after paying for shelter and food. They had little choice as to where they lived. They tended to drift to the least attractive and least sought-after areas — the nineteenth-century ghettoes where law and order was in the hands of the strongest and most cunning. There were many parts in Britain's large cities where the police accepted they had little power. In these parts were found the worst housing conditions, the most persistent diseases, the worst social misery, all unrelieved by any hope of improvement. Today, although there are still "grey" areas in many large towns and cities, there is not the great mass of suffering within the overcrowded, unhealthy slums which was the dominant feature of the inner areas of any nineteenth-century industrial town. Now there is adequate, sometimes attrac-

tive, low-income housing all around, whole districts of it. The contrast between the two varieties of landscape is enormous, and, like every other feature of the environment, there is an explanation for the changes.

Guide to further study

This chapter and study introduce a series of sources and approaches which are common to many of the following chapters. The most important of these are:

(a) The use of maps.
The most useful maps for urban study are the Ordnance Survey 1:2500 and 1:1250, commonly called the "twenty-five inch to the mile" and "fifty inch to the mile". These maps, or more properly plans, are widely available for all large towns and many smaller ones. Because they are at so large a scale they can be used for plotting growth in great detail. They can be used for measuring the areas of buildings and other features and from this for measuring densities. They also clearly show the arrangement of buildings, the functions of major buildings and details such as the width of streets. It is very difficult for the Ordnance Survey to keep pace with the rate of change in many urban areas and so the plans are often out-of-date, showing features which may have disappeared five years previously. While this can prove a problem if a correct map is required, it means that even the plans at present published are historical records and can be used for studying change.

If we wish to study early periods of growth and the features of a town, then we have to turn to County Record Offices, or possibly to Central Libraries. Copies, or originals, of local town maps can be seen, and copies may be used for work, e.g. number of houses, area of occupied zone. In the latter half of the eighteenth century and the first half of the nineteenth, most of the urban areas we see today were being mapped because of Enclosure Awards or in relation to tithes. For example, the Tithe Commutation Act of 1836, which changed tithes into a rent charge, resulted in a large-scale map of areas affected, showing owners and occupiers of land, the maps at a scale of between thirteen and twenty-five inches to the mile.

Large-scale Ordnance Survey plans appear in the 1840s, many at scales which are now obsolete and therefore make precise physical comparison difficult. From 1843 publication began of town plans on scales of 1:1056 (sixty inches to the mile), 1:528 (ten feet to the mile) and 1:500 (roughly ten and a half feet to the mile). The 1:1056 were published for towns of over 4,000 inhabitants for the area north of a line from Preston to Hull, and were mostly completed by 1855. The larger scales came a little later but some remained unpublished.

Information on particular plans and their availability is contained in *The Historian's Guide to Ordnance Survey Maps*, reprinted from *Amateur Historian* with additional material, published by the National Council of Social Service, 1965. By 1894 these scales had disappeared, replaced by the ones used today.

(b) Sources of social statistics.

The most widely available material comes from the Census of Population taken every ten years since 1801, except for 1941. These are full Censuses, but there are also sample statistics based on a section of the total population and now taken at the mid-point between the full Censuses.

Information from the early periods is less detailed than in modern collections but there are useful sections on inhabited/uninhabited houses and occupation from 1801 onward. Occupational information becomes more precise by 1831 and 1841 and includes birthplace. The 1971 Census gives statistics on number of living rooms per dwelling, supply of hot and cold water, presence of bath, sink, WC, cooking stove and gives the type of building. However, most Censuses are available only as digests where the statistics are presented for census districts. County Record Offices have copies of the original enumeration sheets, taken on a house-to-house basis, but the last date which is available to the general public is 1871. These data sheets do give an enormous amount of information on a personal basis, including occupation, ages of members of the family and places of birth. Occupations can also be obtained from local directories (see the guide to further study, chapter two).

A very useful publication is *Social Trends*, published by HMSO, which appears yearly now and contains details of past and present trends in population, housing and home facilities, leisure activities, journey to work patterns and many more.

(c) The third of these important sources is not a publication but an activity — observation. There is really no substitute for observation as a means of obtaining material. Of course you have to know what you are looking for, where it might be and what you are going to do with the information when you get it, and for this preliminary reading is necessary and maps and plans may have to be consulted. But to understand what the sources are concerned with, to appreciate the details they emphasize, you have to do some walking and sightseeing. From this comes recording, analysis of the information *you* have gathered and evaluation of how *you* think it relates to what you previously believed.

There are two other reasons for moving out into the urban scene. Firstly, in going to see one particular feature, it often becomes clear that another factor is closely associated with it, or a series of elements all interrelate. In the next study working-class housing is the topic, but housing is only one part of the whole environment. Inspection of what remains of the nineteenth-century housing for the poor must include its associations, the narrow streets, lack of open spaces. The second reason is that as many of the components of the urban landscape are commonplace, sometimes there is little information on them, at least at a local level. They are so familiar people take them for granted. They also disappear very easily. Again, with the example of housing for the poor, few local Councils preserve nineteenth-century slums, indeed, they wish to pull them down as quickly as possible. So, if you wish to see what this housing was like, how people lived a hundred years ago in large towns, you have to get out into the older areas and get out quickly. Why aren't there more preservation orders on small numbers of back-to-backs and terraces, so that in a hundred years people will be able to see them, rather than just read about them?

Bibliography:

For the history of urban development, both in terms of growth and importance:

W. G. Hoskins, *The Making of the English Landscape* (Hodder, 1972/Penguin, 1972)
G. Burke, *Towns in the Making* (Arnold, 1971)
A. E. J. Morris, *A History of Urban Form* (Godwin, 1972)
L. Mumford, *The City in History* (Penguin, 1973)

Social and economic conditions in the growing urban areas are described in:

R. Roberts, *The Classic Slum* (Manchester University Press, 1971)
E. R. Pike, *Human Documents of the Industrial Revolution in Britain* (Unwin, 1966)
M. Bruce, *The Coming of the Welfare State* (Batsford, 1961 & 1971)
A. Fried & R. Elman (eds), *Charles Booth's London* (Hutchinson, 1969)
L. Mumford, *The Culture of Cities* (Secker & Warburg, 1938)
A. Briggs, *Victorian Cities* (Penguin, 1968)
M. D. George, *London Life in the Eighteenth Century* (Penguin, 1966)
F. Engels, *The Condition of the Working Class in England* (Unwin, 1971/Panther, 1969)
E. Gauldie, *Cruel Habitations. A history of working-class housing, 1780–1918* (Unwin, 1974)

Many writers of fiction in the nineteenth century gave vivid accounts of urban conditions in their own time. Charles Dickens is probably the best example.

Study 1 Growth of low-income housing

The growth of the towns

Life for the poor in 1800 was short and unpleasant. This applies particularly to those living in the new industrial towns; in the market and county towns a community still provided some help for its less-fortunates. The worst conditions were in the largest towns and cities. In Liverpool, in 1840, the expectation of life at birth of a labourer's child was 15 years and sixty-two per cent of all children died before the age of five. In Bethnal Green, the poorest district in London, the expectation of life was sixteen years. Many of the nineteenth-century industrial towns grew mainly through immigration. Natural increase of the poor was low, in spite of the large number of children born. High birth rates were matched by high death rates and, in time of epidemic, the latter might be higher than the former. In spite of this, people poured into the towns, either drawn by the chance of work, or perhaps driven by agricultural changes which left them landless or unemployed. The eighteenth and early nineteenth centuries saw a great wave of land enclosures as landowners enlarged their fields and farms. Often this meant that the agricultural workers were forced from their homes, no longer needed as farming became technically more advanced. The scale of these movements was often enormous. The 1851 Census showed that London had gained 330,000 new immigrants in the previous ten years, equivalent to seventeen per cent of the 1841 population. In many cases the towns, which had changed little in size for hundreds of years, found their population doubled or trebled within a decade. Within them, the immigrant poor lived where they could, in cellars, barns, stables, crammed together a family to a room. Even when they were employed, they could not save, and there was no chance for them to buy land, or houses. The building, by private landlords, of houses for rent was slow to develop, and what we now call local authority, or council housing was non-existent. Even if the local authorities had wished to build houses, areas such as Manchester were not classified as towns in 1830 and had no power to provide services.

How the poor lived

Gradually, large-scale, low-cost housing was developed, and it had very obvious characteristics. The primary object of the landowners and builders was to cram as many dwellings as possible into the space at their disposal. The town fields and heaths were bought and built upon, progressively enlarging the urban areas. A series of building forms was used, the earliest being the court. A plan of a typical organization is shown in Figure 13 and their con-

Above: Fig. 12 Entrance to a cellar dwelling. Dated 1766, this would lead to a small room with an earth floor, which would be flooded in times of heavy rain. It was in places like these that three out of ten children died before the age of twelve months.

fined nature is obvious. They were an extension of a medieval building style, but in the case of the early speculative builders, their attraction was not the close sense of community which might evolve, but their low cost. Chiefly this was because of their high density, which made the cost of land per dwelling very small, and the lack of road costs. Building in a closed court form meant that the interior area could be left unpaved, and there need be no connection with the existing road system. In the early expansion of the towns, most low-cost housing ended in a *cul-de-sac*. No early nineteenth-century courts remain, but there has been sufficient written about them to show that they were generally poorly-built, overcrowded, ill-lit and insanitary. A typical court would be entered from the street by way of a narrow, covered passage. Inside would be a small, open area about three metres wide, with between six and twenty houses facing one another. The houses would be of two or three rooms, one for each floor, each between about $2\frac{1}{2}$ and $3\frac{1}{2}$ metres square (about 27 to 38 square feet). There would be no running water, the toilet arrangements would consist

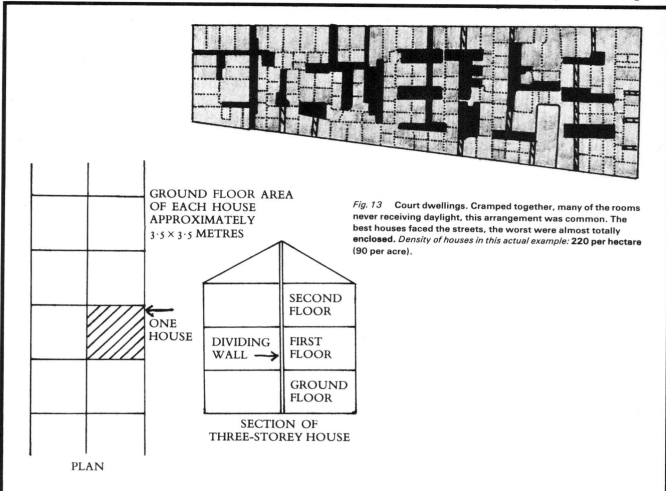

GROUND FLOOR AREA
OF EACH HOUSE
APPROXIMATELY
3·5 × 3·5 METRES

ONE
HOUSE

Fig. 13   **Court dwellings. Cramped together, many of the rooms
never receiving daylight, this arrangement was common. The
best houses faced the streets, the worst were almost totally
enclosed.** *Density of houses in this actual example:* **220 per hectare
(90 per acre).**

SECOND
FLOOR

DIVIDING
WALL →

FIRST
FLOOR

GROUND
FLOOR

SECTION OF
THREE-STOREY HOUSE

PLAN

of an earth closet, little more than a hole in the ground, and
it would not be unusual for a room to be shared by more
than one family. The open part of the court was no village
green. Unpaved and undrained, it collected stagnant water
and all the refuse of the houses. As the closets were emptied,
dunghills piled up and they were allowed to grow until
they dominated the neighbourhood, especially the atmosphere. When they had grown to sufficient size, they were
sold, to be carted away to farms. Until the second half
of the century when guano (concentrations of bird
droppings, from South America) was imported, these
dunghills were a chief source of fertilizer for the farmers
who worked around the towns.

The courts were built back-to-back, that is the external
walls of the houses were shared and there was no rear
entrance. By the 1830s this arrangement was extended into a
terrace form. This was particularly true where the land was
owned in large areas. If only small areas were available then
single houses might be built, or a large number of dwellings
concentrated into the area. The type of land tenure often
greatly influenced the building form. In many cases the land
was made available on a leasehold basis, reverting back to
the landowner after a specified time. If the land was on a
thirty-year lease, there was no incentive for the developer
to build houses which would be long-lasting, as he would
lose control of them at the end of the period. However,
where a major landowner also acted as developer, there was
usually more control and care over the design and
construction of the buildings. In freehold areas, where the
full title to the land could be bought, small parcels of land
were built up at very high densities and it was here that the
worst overcrowding usually occurred.

The terrace became the dominant building form from the
1830s onward, firstly in the back-to-backs, moving through
its variations, such as tunnel backs, to the late Victorian
terrace which can still be seen today. These developments
were improvements but they were not accomplished easily.
For most builders and developers the lowest standards and
quickest profit were the criteria of success and they did not
change their views until forced to.

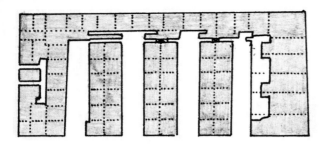

Fig. 14   Houses for rich and poor. These plans are of two sets of buildings, each constructed in the 1830s but very different. The terraces are (left) an improvement on the back-to-backs, each at least receiving some light. The suburban villa (below) was only a kilometre away in distance but a world away in comfort. *Density of housing:* Terrace: 150 per hectare (60 per acre) Villa: 2 per hectare.

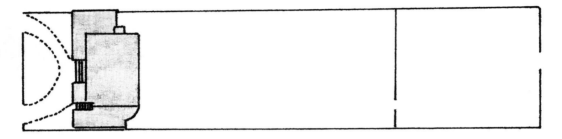

The first improvements and the Public Health Acts

It became obvious by the middle of the century that there were serious defects in the housing of the poor. The industrial towns were described by most commentators as concentrations of filth, misery, disease and vice. In 1847 the Statistical Society of London surveyed Church Lane, St Giles, near Oxford Street. Below is their description of one of the houses, very typical of conditions which were to be found in any large British city.

"House No. 4 – Two Parlours, on Ground Floor
Size of front room, 14ft long, 13ft broad, 6ft high; size of windows, 3ft 4in by 2ft 2in. Size of back-room, 11ft 2in long, 9ft 4in broad, less than 6ft in height; 1 window with 4 whole panes; rent paid, 5s 6d weekly for 2 rooms; under-rent paid, 3d per night each adult; time occupied, 2 years; number of families, 5; comprising 4 males above 20, 9 females above 20, three of them single, 2 males under 20, 4 females under 20; total 19. Number of persons ill, 2; deaths in 1847, 1, measles. Country, Irish; trade, dealers and mendicants. State of rooms and furniture, bad, dirty; state of windows, 6 whole panes, and 10 broken. Number of beds, 6; number of bedsteads, 6.

The door of this room opens into the yard, 6 feet square, which is covered over with night soil; no privy, but there is a tub for the accommodation of the inmates; the tub was full of night soil. These are nightly lodging-rooms. In the front room one girl, 7 years old, lay dead, and another was in bed with its mother, ill of the measles."

Although the dead girl was not a typical daily feature of the average dwelling, in times of epidemics, such as measles, death was a familiar element in every household.

There was little control on standards of housing for the poor, little knowledge of the causes of the epidemic diseases which swept through the towns, and, once the middle classes were able to move away from the centres, little concern for the poor. There were some passionate advocates of improvement, such as Edwin Chadwick (1801–90), first Secretary to the Poor Law Commissioners, who attempted to shock authorities into some degree of action by publicizing the statistics of death and disease among the poor. He, and his supporters, had an uphill battle against property owners and those who thought that the poor produced their own conditions, like a pig in its filth. Two factors made housing reform a matter for respectable concern, moral health and epidemics.

Within the courts and alleys, disease was endemic, ever-present. Filth in the houses, courts and streets bred rats, and the lice which fed on them brought typhus. Tuberculosis, smallpox and diphtheria spread rapidly because of overcrowding. These factors were rarely a problem with the middle and upper classes and they could ignore these problems of the slums. They could not ignore typhoid and cholera. Until 1849 it was possible to believe that these great urban killers, which were not confined to the poor and overcrowded, were transmitted by smell. The middle classes complained of the "putrid miasmata" of the poor areas, but believed that if one could not smell the stench, one could not catch the disease. The reasons why they were so preoccupied with smell can be seen from this description of one of the poorest districts in London.

Fig. 15   Best quality back-to-backs. Best quality because they remain. Most of the normal, less well-built ones have vanished. In these houses there is no backyard for drying clothes, so the clothes-horse is outside the front door. In many the dust-bin would be outside as well. Communal toilets would be across the street.

Fig. 16   A terraced court. A *cul-de-sac*, built in the 1850s. The only light comes through the gap of the back entry. The central channel, or kennel, was the only means of surface drainage, and virtually guaranteed that the area would flood. Demolished in 1974.

"That part of Three Colts Lane which is without a sewer is very dirty and the gutters full of dirt and fluid filth. There is always a great deal of fever in this lane. Parallel to, and north of, Arch 81 of the railway, and abutting on the lane, is a small pool of pasty, putrescent filth and a collection of garbage. On the south side of the same arch is an open, black, filthy ditch, which is from eight to ten feet wide, and from three to four hundred feet long. The uncovered privies at the back of North Street drain their soil into it; the soil has accumulated, and with decomposing cats and dogs, and refuse, which are thrown into it, since Lambs Fields have been occupied, produce an odour of the most abominable character."

Hector Gavin, *Sanitary Ramblings*, 1848, p. 20.

In 1849 Dr John Snow (1813–58) proved that cholera in a London district was related to polluted water supply. With no private water supply, the poor relied on wells or pumps. Most poor-quality houses had earth closets, with no means of carrying the waste to the few sewers, which, in the early nineteenth century were often built only to carry away excess surface water from the roads. The human waste, accumulating in pits, and forbidden in many cases from being discharged into the sewers, seeped through the ground and polluted underground water supplies. When this happened, the rich and famous got no immunity by living away from the slums. Prince Albert died of typhoid in 1861. It became in the interests of the upper classes to

support housing reform, and, after each outbreak of cholera, support grew. *The Times* called cholera "the best of all sanitary reformers, it overlooks no mistake". With the increasing scale of urban development, the pressures increased. The River Thames, by the 1850s, had become such an open sewer that the smell filled the new Houses of Parliament, a powerful stimulus to legislation.

The question of moral behaviour also provided a focus rallying many eminent Victorians to support reform and control of housing for the poor. To these Victorians, the obviously loose morals of the working classes, their drunkenness and lack of respect for marriage, were related to their overcrowded conditions, where privacy was impossible. Jack the Ripper lent a hand to reform, when after his savage murders of prostitutes in Central London, delicate Victorian minds were shocked by descriptions of his victims' home and social conditions.

The results, both of individual agitation and growing public pressure, were the Public Health Acts. A list of the major Acts dealing with health and housing is on page 21. They slowly built up a body of control which compelled local authorities to improve the low-cost housing within their area. The progress was slow because landlords and builders objected to curbs on their activities, and often their opinions were well-supported in Parliament and in local Councils. Some of the more prominent of the objectors were called "Defenders of the Filth".

Below: Fig. 17 **Water supply. In many areas the dates on these fountains show when piped water first arrived in the district.**

Table I   Main Acts dealing with Public Health and Housing in the Nineteenth Century

Date	Name of Act	Details of the Act and its effects on the urban area
*1817·	Michael Angelo Taylor's Act	Referred to the City of London, Westminster and Southwark and dealt with improving streets and paving.
*1833	Burgh Police Act	Gave Scots authorities power to appoint Police Commissioners in charge of lighting and cleansing.
1837	Public Health Act	Gave power to control surface drains.
1840	Small Tenements Bill	Defeated in Parliament but was the first main attempt to control house building. Attempted to forbid houses built below ground level, back-to-backs and those without drains.
1846	Nuisances Removal Act	Gave powers for the cleansing of towns but no special authorities to control it. In the same year Britain's first Medical Officer of Health appointed in Liverpool.
1848	Public Health Act	Powers to establish Boards of Health with control over water supply, cleansing, draining and paving. Medical Officers of Health could be appointed. Boards of Health could forbid use of cellars as dwellings and stop new building if it had inadequate drains and toilets.
1851	Lodging Houses Act	Local authorities able to inspect lodging houses and to erect and operate them.
1855	Nuisances Removal Act	This defined overcrowding in houses as a public "nuisance" and gave power to MOH to enter premises.
1858	Local Government Act	Power to local authorities to make bye-laws to control building.
1858	Amendment to Public Health Act of 1848	Gave power to forbid the building of new back-to-backs.
1866	Sanitary Act	Required local authorities to supply water to townships. Owners of houses could be forced to connect drains to sewers or covered cess-pits.
1866	Labouring Classes Dwelling Houses Act	Establishment of Public Works Loan Commissioners who were able to make loans for dwelling houses. Led to building of "model dwellings".
1868	Artisans and Labourers Dwelling Act (Torrens Act)	Owners of houses should keep them in good repair in sanitary matters. If not local authority could enforce repair or rebuilding.
1872	Public Health Act	Medical Officer of Health compulsory. Important because they were the chief officials concerned with enforcing standards of health and housing.
1875	Artisans and Labourers Dwellings Improvement Act (Cross Act)	Dealt with insanitary areas which needed clearing and rebuilding. Local authorities given powers to acquire housing, clear it, draw up schemes for improvement and lease the land or build new houses themselves.
1875	Public Health Act	This was the most important of the Acts in its effects. Almost all of the legislation until now had been very permissive, allowing local authorities to carry out improvements, if they wished. This Act was still, in many ways, permissive, but there were much stronger powers for authorities who wished to use them. In every area, officers of Health and Sanitary Inspectors were to be appointed. A Government department, the Local Government Board, was to be responsible for public health and the Poor Law, with a Chief Medical Officer in charge. Compelled local authorities to build sewage works. Power to build isolation hospitals for infections diseases. Gave power for local authorities to (a) Name streets. (b) Light streets. (c) Make building bye-laws for local use. (d) Repair streets. (e) Set new building lines where houses or other buildings demolished. Allowed the widening of previous narrow roads. (f) Enforce regulations referring to standards of light in houses (connected with minimum width of streets) and amount of yard space at rear of houses, which was to be not less than 14 square metres (150 sq ft). The Act set into motion local action which resulted in much of the nineteenth-century, low-income housing we see now. The pace of acceptance varied from town to town but the features of the nineteenth-century terraced landscape, with its amenity bays, garden "areas", outside toilets, backyards, dates from this Act.
1886	Housing of the Working Classes Act	Followed from the Royal Commission on the Housing of the Working Classes set up in 1884. The main effect was that in 1886 Treasury loans were available to local authorities to build houses, if they wished to.
1888	Public Health Amendment (Buildings and Streets) Act	Prohibited the extension of buildings beyond the line of those on either side.
1888	Local Government Act	Reconstructed the basis of local Government and gave greater powers to authorities.
1890	Housing Act	Authorities given powers to demolish single insanitary houses. Able to build (single) houses for occupation.
1890	Public Health (Amendment) Act	Authorities able to control flushing water to toilets. Also dealt with the minimum height of rooms, structure of floors, hearths and staircases. Forbade the construction of dwellings over privy or cesspool. First Act covering the actual construction of houses.

Although the Acts became stronger as the century passed, there were still great problems to be solved at the end of the period. Mainly this was because the legislation was permissive and few councils acted upon it. An example of the slow rate of change is that although attempts were made to outlaw back-to-backs from 1840, they were not legally prohibited in all of Britain until 1936 when the Housing Act made their construction a criminal offence.

For this reason, the effect of the Acts varies from place to place. Those towns with the most obvious problems often led in adopting their own model building bye-laws.

* These first Acts only applied to specified parts of the country.

Bye-law houses and model dwellings

Not all nineteenth-century housing improvement was the result of long and bitter struggle. A few philanthropic factory owners, believing that their workers had a right to decent conditions, built "model dwellings". Robert Owen's New Lanark, begun in 1792, was the first of these, and later in the period came Titus Salt's Saltaire (1854), Price's village at Bromborough (1854), and the most famous examples Port Sunlight (1888), and Bournville (1895). These were integrated settlements, including not only housing of above-average quality for its time, but also churches, schools, clubs, wash-houses, parks, hospitals and even art galleries. They became the forerunners of what we now call the Welfare State, where employers accept a degree of responsibility for the condition of life of their workers. However, they were exceptional for their time, and most employers found it easier to leave the problem to the growing concern of the State.

By 1890 the standard dwelling for the poor was the bye-law terrace, still remaining in large numbers. Figure 18 shows an example of this type of urban landscape. The changes which have resulted from Public Health legislation can be seen clearly. Gone are the unpaved courts, now there is an eight-metre-wide road, allowing sunlight to reach the lower rooms; the Victorians were great believers in the curative properties of the sun. The window areas have increased and the "amenity bay" has become a common feature since 1875. Mass-produced sash windows give greater ventilation, and the small garden "area" provides a private zone of greenery. Inside, the houses are four- or six-roomed, still small, but with a cold-water tap, and some of those built after 1870 have a back-boiler for heating water. The kitchen range became widely used after 1860, and families could cook all their own food, instead of relying on street vendors as they had done previously. After 1890, all new houses had closets supplied with running water, mostly built in the back yard and replacing the former systems of communal privies, which had each been shared by perhaps twenty or thirty families.

The terrace was the standard dwelling in most industrial towns, although there were exceptions. Many local councils had built tenements on the Scottish model, but the development of high-rise housing was hindered partly by poor building technique, but also because, until 1851, a tax was levied on the number of windows in a building. Single buildings containing large numbers of windows paid high rates, unless they were obviously built for a large number of families. So the English tenements were designed with galleries and staircases, giving separate access, which showed the building to be a series of independent dwellings. It also made them an expensive method of providing housing. After 1850, they became very much associated with "model dwellings", built by a series of charitable Trusts who put up cheap housing for certain sections of the

working classes. Although they portrayed themselves as charities, they made a quite acceptable profit on their properties and it was only the more prosperous of the workers who could afford to live in their buildings. Unfortunately, many of these "model dwellings" looked very gloomy, which did not help to spread their use. The efforts of the most notable of these groups, the Peabody Trust, have been described as "humanitarian in its pretensions, yet depressing in its results".

The twentieth century

In spite of the improvements brought about by legislation, there was still an enormous gap between the housing standards of different social groups. Many local authorities ignored the Acts, for throughout the nineteenth century, most were merely permissive, allowing the authority to control buildings, *if they wished*. Many did not. For example, although new back-to-backs could be forbidden from 1858 onwards, they were still being built in Leeds up until the 1930s. Many councils appointed only part-time

Below: Fig. 18   **Bye-law terraces. Superior terraces built between 1890 and 1908. The backyards can be seen clearly and also the combined coal-shed and toilet, where they were built. The ones at the foot of the diagram have a marked amenity bay projecting beyond the building line.** *Density of housing:* **95 per hectare (40 per acre). This was a lower density than most bye-law properties.**

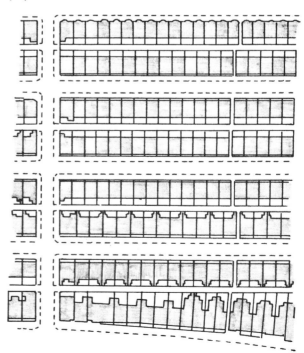

Medical Officers of Health, who were the officials responsible for the examination of housing. However, housing conditions did everywhere improve, aided by a lessening of the rate of population growth, but there was still far too little housing available. Very little private building for the working-class market was carried out between 1890 and 1914. In 1919, it was estimated that 600,000 houses were needed to provide merely adequate housing standards for the population. The great shortage was in low-income housing — the other income groups provided a more secure market for house builders. To cope with this need and to provide "a land fit for heroes", the Government felt it necessary to introduce the 1919 Housing and Town Planning (Addison's) Act. This made Local Authorities produce schemes for house building and gave financial assistance towards them. It was the start of "council housing" which now makes up a large proportion of our housing stock.

A new building style developed, breaking with old patterns. The new housing was to be at a much-reduced density, three-bedroomed, with kitchen, bath and garden. New layouts were introduced and the semi-detached appeared, arranged in crescents and closes. Local councils built over 200,000 houses between 1919 and 1925, planned at no more than thirty to the hectare (twelve to the acre), hopefully having no more than seventy people in that area. Since that time, local authority housing has multiplied, spreading throughout the urban area, creating peripheral suburban estates and renewing the inner areas. During the 1950s and 1960s the rising price of land led to the development of large sections of high-rise buildings, following on from the municipal tenements of the period between the two World Wars.

Tall blocks of flats have not proved popular. Young children have no gardens or play-areas, many people from terraced houses miss the street as a focus and meeting-place and breakdowns in the lift systems, not uncommon, can make life unbearable for the elderly. In both high-rise and

Below: Fig. 19   **Model dwellings built in 1868, following the Labouring Classes Dwelling Houses Act. These are model tenements which have been continually improved and until recently were still in use. One of the first "council" houses in Britain.**

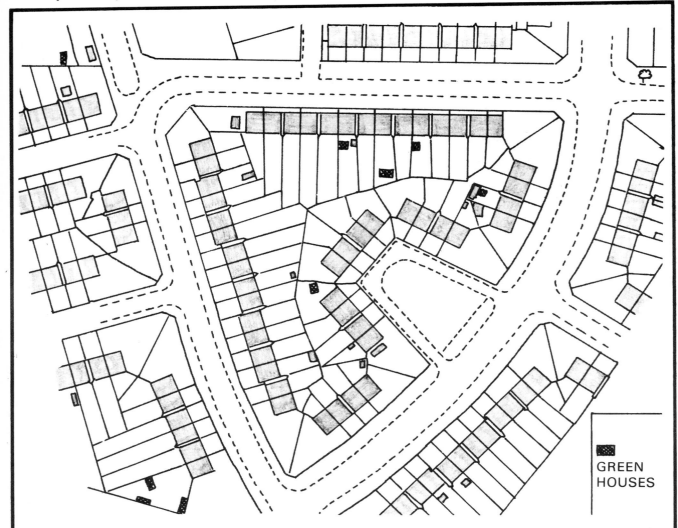

GREEN
HOUSES

the longer, lower "deck dwellings", lifts, stairs and passageways provide plenty of opportunity for vandalism and petty larceny, although the root cause is not the design of the buildings, only aided by it. On Merseyside, in 1976, officials are pondering what to do with two blocks of flats, Eldon and Oak Gardens in Birkenhead. They have had so many social problems associated with them that no one will live in them and one solution being considered, which would be unique in this country in respect of twenty-year-old buildings, is that they should be demolished. Recent construction has returned to a low level, often in a short terrace form, arranged more intricately than the long, monotonous rows of the nineteenth century. Council housing has not been an unmixed blessing. It has produced some dull and ugly buildings and, in some cases, new sets of social problems, but there are now no large areas of appalling slums within our cities and the poor, although perhaps less healthy than most, no longer have death rates two or three times those of other social groups.

Above: Fig. 20   **Inter-war council estate. Typical development of its time, with crescent forms and "closes". Lots of open space but very little of it is public. Housing is in blocks, with runnels through to the back. Notice the solitary tree in the top right.** *Density of housing:* **25 per hectare (10 per acre).**

Right: Fig. 21   **High-rise. A major feature of recent development, tower blocks were thought of as an answer to high land values and the need for recreation space. This one is twenty-two storeys high. The wind effects they create can blow down young trees and destroy football games.**

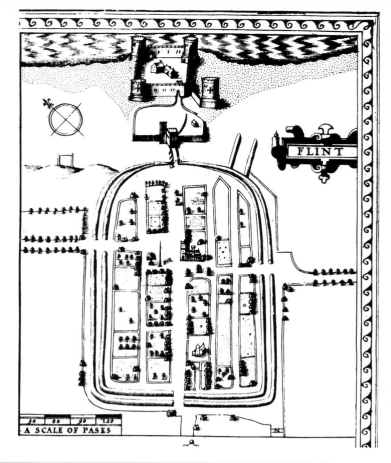

A SCALE OF PASES

Left: Fig. 22   Medieval Flint, a map by John Speed from his *Theatre of the Empire of Great Britaine*, published in 1611.

Below: Fig. 23   An aerial photograph of modern Flint.

4 The transport revolution

In the medieval town there was little need for broad, regular street patterns, as there was little wheeled traffic. The spaces between the buildings were lines of communication rather than transportation. People were more important than vehicles. Street patterns in medieval England were irregular with few straight lines. Part of this may have been due to the need for protection against the wind, for staggered patterns would break its force.

A few towns had an exceptionally regular plan, some owing their arrangement to Roman organization. Another group were the bastide towns, built in the Middle Ages to support and supply the armies stationed along the Welsh Marches. Within them the main streets were built at a standard width of 25 feet (8 metres), minor roads at 16 feet (5 metres) and rear lanes at 8 feet (2½ metres). Figure 22 shows a plan by John Speed (1542–1629) of the bastide town Flint, drawn in 1611. The photograph in Figure 23 shows a modern view of the town. The road pattern remains, still dividing the area into a series of quarters, corresponding to medieval *insulae*.

Generally streets remained narrow until the sixteenth century when spoke-wheeled vehicles became common in the towns. As travel became faster the old road patterns became uneconomic and obstructive. As government became more centralized in London, there was a still greater need for a fast and efficient transport system which would, naturally, focus on the capital. Improvements could be justified in terms of the encouragement of economic progress or, in a more sinister manner, because of a wish to move troops quickly around the country. The British did not go as far as the French where, in the 1870s, Baron Haussmann (1809–91) drove great boulevards through the remnants of medieval Paris, so that the military could deal quickly with potential revolutionaries. Gradually street widths in Britain widened and became standardized. Once again, the greatest changes came in the nineteenth century. Road improvement quickened through the work of the turnpike trusts but, for a period of half a century, railways dominated towns and their features. It has been said that railways had more radical consequences for the characteristics of the large mid-Victorian towns than any other single factor.

While within the urban areas the movement of individuals and the transport of goods remained tied to pedestrian or horse-drawn means, the developing railways carved a national network through town and country. From the 1840s to the 1890s every major town grew a web of lines and stations. As trains were noisy and dirty, it was arranged that they would be routed through the working-class areas and whole districts were razed to make way for the track. By the 1890s most of the damage had been done and, during this century, there has been little extension of the network. Where it has grown, it has sometimes done so underground, a practice begun by the Metropolitan Railway in London, opened in 1863. Railways are now far less of a factor in the urban landscape than they used to be. Many old stations now serve different uses, acting as car parks or as sites for new offices. The lines are often unused, as Victorian cities often had more lines and stations than they merited. Different railway companies would compete for dominance, each building their own facilities, so that now, when railways have lost their supremacy, the duplicated features lie idle. Although the "age of the railway" has passed, its position having been taken by the road system, it has had long-lasting effects on our urban structure, particularly in the larger cities. The following passage deals with the impact of railway building upon London. It shows how the explosion of new transport facilities influenced the size and arrangement of our largest urban area.

"In London itself the railways jolted the existing social and economic structure into a new pattern, as indeed they did in greater or lesser degree in every great town throughout the country. In the City itself and its immediate environs, the resident population dispersed itself outwards to the less cramped surroundings of the new suburbs. The centre became the area where Londoners worked, in shops, warehouses, offices, banks

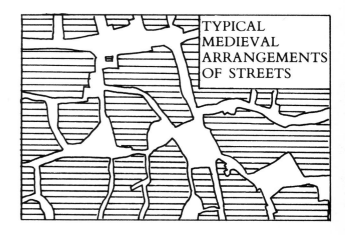

TYPICAL MEDIEVAL ARRANGEMENTS OF STREETS

Left: Fig. 24   Nineteenth-century industrial street. Two-and-a-half metres wide, enough to allow the metal-rimmed wheels of carts to reach the stone flags at the edge of the surface. No drains, and in the middle, granite setts.

Right: Fig. 25   Obsolete roads. The one on the right is of the 1830s, wide enough to allow one carriage through. Even as a suburban road it proves inefficient and is by-passed.

and a few specialized manufacturing industries, but where few except the poor, dependent on casual employment and unable to pay to travel to work, still lived, often in conditions of the utmost squalor and degradation. With the advent of workmen's cheap fares on the railways after 1864, the more prosperous sections of the working classes could afford to move outwards too, and very gradually the separation of work and home assumed its huge modern proportions and made it perhaps the greatest of all twentieth-century problems of town planning."

Francis Sheppard, *London 1808–1870: The Infernal Wen*, 1971, p. 119.

As railway building slowed, road building accelerated. The development of the internal combustion engine and its use in road vehicles from 1885 opened a flood-gate of activity. The motor car has since had a dominating influence on urban characteristics. In the nineteenth century traffic density within towns was low, horse-drawn vehicles had a limited size and carrying capacity and the distance they worked over was, in general, very short. The first horse-drawn omnibuses, the "Shillibeers" of London, began operating in 1829, carried twenty passengers, but operators restricted their use to distances of up to five miles (8 kilometres). Beyond this they were little competition to the railways. Events might have been different if the steam carriages of the 1830s had been developed as a serious competitor to railways. Using the normal roads they showed up well in a series of test runs. However, many

turnpike trusts were renewed at this time and most of them were violently opposed to steam transport on the roads. High tolls were introduced in an effort to curb its growth. In some cases the tolls were as much as seven times that of comparable horse-drawn traffic. The attack succeeded but railways were the main beneficiaries. Heavy goods traffic moved almost entirely to their rapid service.

The roads remained the preserve of the horse carriage until 1869, when bicycles began to appear in some numbers. These were viewed as unnecessary intrusions and, besides the discomfort of riding on solid tyres, the unfortunate cyclist was obliged to ring his bell continuously. The few steam carriages that remained had to contend with the Red Flag Act of 1865 which restricted their speed to two miles per hour in towns, and demanded that a man with a red flag, or lantern, walk sixty yards (55 metres) ahead of the vehicle. It is not surprising that there was little commercial pressure for the improvement of the roads. In the towns heavy rain made them into quagmires, tales were told of servants who, sent out on an errand, disappeared in the mud, never to be seen again. The boot-scraper was an essential part of Victorian door furniture and many homeless children earned their livings by sweeping street crossings. They waited, with their brooms, for the rich and well-dressed and swept the dirt from their way as they crossed the street.

A hundred years later we have a road system which, in theory, makes possible fast, all-weather transport within the urban area. This road network is changing and growing all the time. As traffic control and information has become more and more complicated, our roadside environment has become most futuristic within the urban area. We think in terms of separating pedestrian and bicycle traffic from the fast-moving vehicle stream, and often the groups are not only physically, but visually distinct, vehicles moving on elevated sections above the life of the town, or diving through subways beneath it. Unlike the medieval town, where main streets were meeting places for discussion and gossip, our urban roads are increasingly separated from the life around them, important for through-traffic but adding nothing to their immediate environment, except carbon monoxide and lead. The differences between the two systems, the old and the new, is a reflection of how urban life has changed and the features we see with us now are the end product of complex technical and economic processes.

Guide to further study

Early editions of large-scale maps can be used to trace the growth of railways within towns and the building of stations. Maps and plans of all historical periods are the source of information on road widths used, for example, to compare figures for minimum widths before and after the passing of Public Health Acts.

County Record Offices will have the records of the turnpike trusts for the area, and possibly of locally-based railway companies. For recent developments the local council is the main point of enquiry. Depending on the size of the urban area, there may be a number of departments who may provide information or advice. The Planning Department, Highways Department or Transportation Services Department should be able to help with questions about new traffic developments and the legislation concerned with transport. Developments planned are often on display in a model form. Some of the larger metropolitan authorities have major plans explaining where and why they want to build new highways. Information from councils is often free and where a charge is made for booklets and pamphlets, it is usually only a small one. Remember that these are working departments and try to make your enquiries specific but also remember that these are publicly-financed offices and you have a right to put reasonable questions to them.

In terms of observation, any town with an old core will have some remnants of the old street pattern, often tucked away at the rear of the major (enlarged?) roads. See them before they, and the buildings around them, are torn down because their narrowness makes them unsuited for modern traffic. In some cases they may be preserved or pedestrianized, but these are the exceptions. Roadworks are an interesting area where you may see, under the tarmac, the setts of previous periods as well as buried tramlines and some of the subterranean features of the urban landscape, pipes, tubes and tunnels.

As well as observing – make records. Examples of features to count are people and traffic. Are pedestrian numbers related to the width of the pavement? Do road widths correspond to differences in PCU totals (see page 33)? See the books on techniques in urban fieldwork at the end of chapter eleven for more details.

Useful books on topics in this section include:

M. Overman, *Roads, Bridges and Tunnels* (Aldus Books, 1968) (a pictorial history of road technology)

A. Bird, *Roads and Vehicles* (Longman, 1969), one of the very useful Industrial Archaeology Series

J. Copeland, *Roads and their Traffic 1750–1850* (David & Charles, 1968)

J. Tetlow & A. Goss, *Homes, Towns and Traffic* (Faber & Faber, 1968) – not exclusively concerned with transport, but deals with a wide range of urban developments

J. R. Kellett *The Impact of Railways on Victorian Cities* (Routledge, 1969)

—— *Roads in Urban Areas* (HMSO, 1966 & 1974).
for a view of the planning of the system.

Study 2 Streetscenes

Roads before the car

Figure 26 shows the construction of an urban motorway. The width and scale of the operation dwarfs the surrounding buildings. This type of road pattern and landscape is our most recent, and like other urban features it is the result of a process of evolution. The changes which have taken place in our paths and roads have been the result of changes in the traffic using them. For hundreds of years the road system remained the same, as forms of transport changed little. Medieval roads were narrow, in some cases only two or three metres, having grown from the paths between houses. In places their width might be determined by agriculture and its requirements, for the transport of agricultural goods and produce was the major type of movement. A $2\frac{1}{2}$-metre (8-foot) passage would allow the movement of a pair of oxen yoked together, and the *cord*, a $1\frac{1}{4}$-metre (4-foot) unit, was a common measurement used in the construction of medieval houses and streets. Stone-paved road surfaces appeared in London from the thirteenth century but, in smaller towns, the roads were often of packed earth. There was, as yet, no separation of pedestrians and vehicles and no pavements, as we know them today.

By the end of the eighteenth century, several changes were noticeable. Streets had become wider to cope with the increased use of wheeled vehicles. This had been stimulated by the widespread appearance of the spoked wheel, which had great advantages over the older, solid one. In the new middle-class areas, and in the reconstructed parts of the old towns, the road widths would now be of a double-carriage width (compare our modern dual-carriageway), usually about five metres. Surfaces had improved, blocks of hard stone, usually granite, were cut to rectangular or chisel shapes of up to 45 centimetres (18 inches), and set in the roadway, separated by compacted earth. Unfortunately wind and rain washed the earth away and the roadway broke up. By the middle of the nineteenth century, regular stone setts, or irregular cobbles, were fixed in cements. Pavements now existed along the street sides, but in many places they were not raised above the road level. To mark the separation of traffic and people at busy junctions posts, which were sometimes old cannons, were used. The great improvements which came about in the last century were begun by the Public Health Acts. Although there were, in all towns, some elegant and gracious streets, the majority were narrow, dirty and dangerous. The Public Health Act of 1838 made newly-constituted urban areas and Boards of Health responsible for the highways in their area. Previously, unless they were administered by the turnpike

Below: Fig. 26   **New roads for old. The motorway used the path of an older road as it is carved through the city. The barrier on the left is put up against noise.**

Opposite page: left (Fig. 27)   **A medieval street. This is a street, Stone Street, at least 400 years old and probably more. Its minimum width is $1\frac{1}{4}$ metres, similar to the old cord; *right (Fig. 28)* early pavements. The first pavements were not elevated from the road as shown in this organization.**

trusts, there was no authority maintaining them. Later, the Local Government Act of 1858 and the Highways Act of 1862 reinforced the responsibilities of the local council. They were able to ignore some of the roads, especially if they were *cul-de-sacs*, by not adopting them as official roads in need of repair, and it is still possible to see unpaved "unadopted" roads and streets in many of our urban areas. The most momentous Public Health Act, that of 1875, included a section requiring all new major roads to be 11 metres (36 feet) wide and all roads in new residential zones to be a minimum of 7·3 metres (24 feet). It was no longer possible to build the type of housing where neighbours could shake hands across the street, while standing by their own front doors.

The impact of motored transport

From the 1880s onward the number of cyclists, and later car, coach and truck users, began to grow fast. Figure 29 shows how, in this century, the number of vehicle registrations increased over the forty years from 1935 to 1975, the period of greatest growth. As more and more people turned to cars and buses for their transport as a result of continued urban expansion, so the road system began to show its limitations. The roads built to the specifications of Telford and Macadam, designed to be pulverized by heavy, slow-moving, cart wheels, broke up with the new methods of transport. The Motor Car Act of 1903 allowed vehicles to travel up to 20 mph (32 kmph), and the increasing speeds threw up small fragments of the road surface. Clouds of dust forced motorists to wear goggles, ladies to use heavy veils and water carts moved about spraying the surface in an attempt to keep down the dust and preserve the road. Vehicle owners applied pressure for improvement on the government of the time, the first "ginger" group being the Road Improvement Association of 1886, formed by the Cyclists' Touring Club. As far back as 1838, wooden blocks had been set in tar to resurface Oxford Street. By the end of the century, the advantages of setting the small stones of the "macadamized" roads in tar were recognized, and tarmacadam appeared. The steamroller, developed in the 1860s combined with the use of asphalt to introduce the construction principles we still see today.

Whose roads?

By 1909, the Government had recognized the inevitability of motor transport, and the Development and Road Improvement Act of that date set up the Road Board. This gave loans to local councils for road development and betterment, financed by a new petrol tax of 3d per gallon and a motor licence duty. From this time onwards, legislation began to organize all the features of the road and roadside and in 1919 a Ministry of Transport was set up. It had already become obvious that more and faster road transport would cause great strain in a system designed for

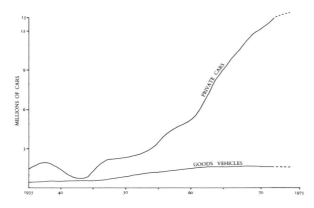

Above: Fig. 29 **Vehicle registrations in the UK 1935–75.**

earlier, slower vehicles. By 1914, nearly all London's omnibuses were petrol driven and the "Golden Age" of the tram was beginning. New forms of road organization developed, trying to speed up the flow of traffic, by separating people and vehicles. From the USA came the Radburn concept, developed in the 1920s by Clarence Stein (born 1882). Its aim was to segregate road users, using a network of freeways and district roads for vehicles and building physically separate walkways for pedestrians. There was also the problem that some of our roads were too narrow to allow free movement of traffic and so the first of our one-way streets, Longacre in London, was created in 1924. Nineteen twenty-six saw the first roundabout, opened in Parliament Square, and the Road Traffic Act of 1930 introduced traffic lights at some intersections.

As well as the surface, size and arrangement of streets, other features of our present surroundings began to appear. Before the 1870s, there was little of what we now call "street furniture". The 1875 Public Health Act gave the power to name streets and provide lighting. Indeed, gas lamps became a legal requirement for every street. Before this time, street lights were confined to the main thoroughfares and the streets of the more affluent and the first compulsory lighting was in the City of Westminster from 1736. Roadside information had been very primitive, confined to information on distance and direction, usually shown on milestones between towns. New types of road sign were needed, large and immediately visible for the new world of rapid transport. There was now no time to stop and read the small print. The first of these new traffic signs was erected by the Cyclists' Touring Club, the Royal Automobile Club and the Automobile Association, a practice still carried on today. In the twentieth century, local and central government produced an ever-increasing number of signs and directions for the motorist. Signs also appeared for the pedestrians, because they too had to be organized. The uncontrolled movement of pedestrians would slow down the flow of vehicles, so they had to be led over bridges, under tunnels or guided across roads with lights and painted patterns. Recently a saner view has emerged in certain town centres where people on foot are given priority and traffic is restricted. Most towns now have some part of their area as a traffic-free pedestrian precinct.

Planning for traffic

The boom in road traffic has led to many conflicts over land-use in the urban areas. Increasingly, the central government has taken over responsibility for organizing the system. Today's roads, pavements and signs are supposed to reflect a fine balance between the demands of the motorist and a powerful lobby of people concerned with the quality of the environment. Each of our urban roads is of a standard size, its width related to the amount of traffic it carries. An increase in the flow of traffic, measured by the small box meters which appear suddenly at the side of roads, brings an up-grading of the section, and so old turnpike becomes a dual-carriageway. Table II shows the system of units used in measuring the traffic flow and table III the relationships between width and potential capacity. Pavements also have their gradings, those in residential districts being of 6 feet wide (2·75 metres), rising to 12–15 feet (3·66–4·57 metres) for areas with a shopping frontage. It is an easy matter to relate pedestrian numbers to pavement width, by comparing the numbers of people using them in a housing district and in a city-centre shopping zone. It is a mistake to believe that what we see around us is arrived at by chance; *almost everything is planned and regulated.* Even the position of traffic signs is controlled, as is the height of the street names on walls.

Roads for the future?

The latest and most obtrusive development in road evolution is the urban motorway. Their construction has been a triumph for the campaigners for road improvement, especially the road haulage users and the motoring organizations. The Cyclists' Touring Club, however, was not as enthusiastic about them as it was about earlier improvements! The huge cost of building these roads, often more than £10 million per kilometre, has kept their growth to a minimum, and they only appear in the largest of our metropolitan areas. They are special roads, needing an Act of Parliament, the Special Roads Act, 1949, as they were the first public roads which are closed to certain types of traffic. The growth of urban motorways has meant the destruction of large parts of some urban areas. What they do not cover with concrete, they isolate. They are the counterpart of the Victorian railways, cutting a great swathe through the city. The advantages of urban motorways for the average town-dweller may diminish in future, in view of our increasing energy problems, and we may see those which have been built become redundant more rapidly than did many railways.

PASSENGER CAR UNITS (PCUs)

These are used in counting traffic density as a way of assessing whether a particular stretch of road is wide enough to cope with its flow of traffic. The figures given are those used for traffic in towns, and differ from those used in rural areas.

Class of vehicle	Value in PCU
Private car, taxi, motor-cycle combination, light goods vehicle (up to 30 cwt – 1,524 kilograms)	1·00
Motor-cycle solo, motor scooter, moped	0·75
Medium or heavy goods vehicle (over 30 cwt unladen weight), horse-drawn vehicle	2·00
Bus, coach, trolley bus, tram	3·00
Pedal cycle	0·33

Above Table II   *Below* Table III

CAPACITIES OF VARIOUS ROADS IN PASSENGER CAR UNITS

Measurements are in PCU per hour. The total of PCU counted should not exceed the capacity of the road.

1. Motorway (three lanes in each direction, 11 metres (36 ft) wide): capacity of 4,500 PCU per hour in one direction.

2. All-purpose road, no access to frontage, no standing vehicles, little cross traffic.

Width (metres)	6·1	6·7	7·3
Width (feet)	20	22	24
Capacity in PCU in both directions	1200	1350	1500

3. All-purpose road with waiting, standing vehicles and junctions.

Width (metres)	6·1	6·7	7·3
Width (feet)	20	22	24
Capacity in PCU in both directions	300/500	450/600	600/750

5 Technology and the architect

If transport improvement has been the major factor in the physical expansion of towns, almost equally important in shaping the urban environment has been technological progress. The growth of the towns has seen waves of successive building styles, sometimes adding to, and sometimes replacing the previous structures. From the first crude shelters, built of sticks and stones, using turf and mud to plug the gaps, we have continually improved our knowledge of design and materials, so that we now have a wide range of style and technique at our disposal. This improvement has been related to economic progress and, as the economy has prospered, so the rate of building change has kept pace with it.

If we take as an example the character of external building materials, then we can see that, in the medieval town, the rate of technical advance was slow. Building style and materials changed very gradually, adaptation taking place as the main raw materials, wood and stone, needed repair. Best English oak, the prime timber of the medieval period, would last for two or three hundred years before needing replacement. Poorer timbers would, however, last a much shorter time. Only a few buildings, usually windmills and watermills, were built entirely of timber. Most were half-timbered, using halved or cleft timbers as opposed to whole logs, making a frame where the spaces were filled with a framework of sticks, or laths, covered with mud or plaster. This "wattle and daub" would need periodical renewal, but, as in the case of fully-timbered buildings, most of the repair work replaced material rather than altering it. Stone was normally more expensive than wood but common houses were sometimes built of rubble stone, fragments crudely fitted together. In grander buildings dressed stones, prepared by masons, would form two outer skins, with rubble filling the space between. These walls could be a metre thick, each of the facing stones carefully fitted and their life span, barring accidents, could be three or four hundred years.

Although town growth was slow, the demand for timber increased rapidly, competition coming from the fast-growing shipbuilding industries and charcoal burning. By the end of the sixteenth century, most of the best timber had been used up. As the supply of best English oak dwindled, poor-quality, short-length timbers had to be used, and eventually the timber-framed house became impracticable. There are, of course, many examples of seemingly fine timber-framed buildings within our towns, often in a "Tudor" black-and-white arrangement. A careful glance can show the wood as machine-cut, serving only as a decorative cladding on what are nineteenth- or twentieth-century reconstructions. The timbers are nailed or bolted on to the building, instead of being secured with pegs as in previous periods. Older material is irregular, being shaped by use of the adze, and it sometimes has carpenters' marks, instructions which made the assembly easier. When modern architects try to create "olde worlde" atmospheres, as in the interiors of some restaurants and public houses, they use plastic beams with a regular patterning, supposed to represent adze marks. While timber disappeared some time ago from town building, stone has had a more variable career. In areas with an abundance of easily-worked stone with a suitable resistance to stress and weather, its use continued into the nineteenth, or even the twentieth century. Elsewhere, the cost of transport and the high wages demanded by skilled masons made stone the privilege of the rich.

The successor for most new building was brick. In the eighteenth and the first half of the nineteenth centuries, every area with surface clay had its local brickworks, producing bricks of a variable quality, usually of poor finish. They were often multicoloured because of impurities in the clay and the lack of controlled heating in the kiln. These defects led to frequent cracking and disintegration. In the eighteenth century, poor-quality bricks were blamed for the collapse of many houses. These local bricks, many with easily-visible variation in size, may be seen in the older buildings of many towns. The standardized brick comes later with cheaper and more efficient transport, certain areas achieving more than a local dominance. The great brick-making area of Britain is the clay belt centred on Bedfordshire, producing over fifty per cent of national brick production. Brick has become the main building material of our towns, which grew when labour was cheap and even huge mills and factories could be completed with an army of bricklayers. Brick was used universally in the buildings of the Industrial Revolution and the scale of the constructions had much to do with the need for mechanizing brick-making processes. For example, during the railway boom, every simple road bridge over the railway used, on average, 300,000 bricks and a tunnel lining would take 14,000,000 for each mile of its length.

However, as the demand grew for stronger, larger, longer buildings, so there was a need for new forms of material. The modern building material is concrete. It has the advantages of speed and strength, and of being able to be moulded into shape and cold set. Like many advances, it was a product of the nineteenth century. Various impure cements were mixed with sand, gravel and water from the 1830s onward but the first true Portland cements came in 1845. In the same year, an eight-storey sugar warehouse was built in Manchester, using iron reinforcing bars set in the concrete. In the 1850s wire mesh was used to give greater strength. Reinforcement made practical the building of high-rise structures in styles not possible before and its use has increased until today it is used for almost every form of urban building. Offices, factories, warehouses, car parks, roads and housing all show its application. We may not recognize immediately its widespread use, because we cover its bareness with more decorative material. Town

centres, in particular, have thin skins of colourful stonework as facing.

Walling is not the only feature of buildings that has undergone advances and changes. Roofs, windows and entrances have all seen drastic modification. Changes are related both to technical improvement and to economic factors. Technical knowledge needs to be available in order to initiate change but the rate at which it proceeds is often explained by economic reasons. In their early stages of development, many techniques are expensive and their general use is often delayed until costs of production can be reduced. In periods of economic depression, there is little incentive to develop new ideas. Most people are naturally conservative, reluctant to change unless there are obvious advantages. In many cases social attitudes have to change before new forms become acceptable. The most obvious

Right: Fig. 30   Local, low-quality bricks. The variation in the colour of these bricks can easily be seen. They also are of different sizes and many have cracked because of uneven firing. The bond is English garden wall, five courses of stretchers to one of headers.

Below: Fig. 31   Rubble-stone walling.

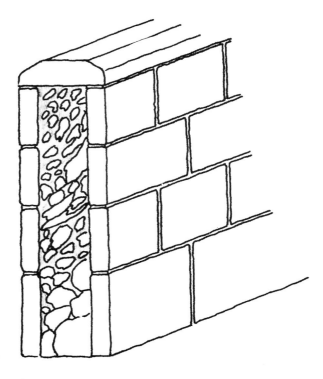

example of this is the dislike many people had of multi-storey, council housing, an attitude which has had a lot to do with the recent reversal of high-rise development. There may also be legal obstacles which slow down the rate of progress. Most of the features which we see around us have been the result of gradual rather than rapid change, evolutionary not revolutionary. The processes operating can be illustrated with reference to the development of one of the more obvious building features – the window. Although the following study is specific, the factors which apply are also relevant to other building characteristics, differing only in degree and precise effect.

Guide to further study

Bibliography: (a) Material
 N. Davey, *A History of Building Material* (Phoenix House, 1961)
 K. Hudson, *Building Materials* (Longman, 1972)
 A. Clifton-Taylor, *A Pattern of English Building* (Batsford, 1972). Very detailed with many regional examples
 N. Davey, *Building in Britain* (Evans, 1963)
     (b) Evolution of building features
 A. Henderson, *The family house in England* (Phoenix House, 1964)
 M. W. Varley, *The House and Home* (Studio Vista, 1971)
 N. Lloyd, *A History of the English House* (Architectural Press, 1931)
 H. Braun, *Old English Houses* (Faber, 1969)

All these books relate to "common" buildings and not to great houses and public buildings. Their styles are dealt with in the bibliography to the next chapter. There has been a recent increase in interest for recording and classifying ordinary (or vernacular) buildings. A book which goes into much detail on building features and characteristics and sets out methods of recording and classification is R. W. Brunskill's *Illustrated Handbook of Vernacular Architecture* (Faber, 1971).

Observation relating to this section is mostly just that. It is only when material and styles are compared with something else, time for example, that explanation of the observed features is necessary. The next chapter is concerned with such an approach.

Below: Fig. 32   **A seventeenth-century house. Built of local materials, crude bricks, stone quoins and windows and thick local flags for the roof.**

Study 3 The window

Glass as a luxury

If we go back two or three thousand years, British houses had no windows as we would recognize them today. Gaps in the branches, stones and sods, which formed the common building would be accidental. Fires would be alight continuously, and smoke was a pressing problem. A hole in the roof would have been the obvious solution, but through this would come rain and snow. Often it was more comfortable to live in the smoke. The alternative was to leave the entrance open, or make holes in the walls. The first of these would let in the cold and, until the development of load-bearing supports, openings in the walls would lead, very quickly, to the collapse of the structure.

The Romans brought glass to Britain, importing it from France, and placing it in iron grilles set within a timber frame. Their stone buildings were strong enough to cope with a number of gaps in the frame. The use of windows and glass was confined to larger buildings, especially those of the conquerors. Glass was little used by Britons until the end of the Anglo-Saxon period, and its use grew with improvements in architecture and national prosperity. Buildings became stronger as masonry techniques improved, and window spaces became common features. Arched, Gothic windows, narrow and built to a point, were the first widespread pattern, still evident in church architecture built in this style. Most of the population could not afford the masonry skills associated with this design, and, in most buildings the openings in the walls were square, or rectangular, supported by stone sills, lintels and mullions.

The first records of glass-making in this country come in the thirteenth century, with Laurence Vitrearius, working at Chiddingford, on the Surrey-Sussex border. The product was expensive, a hand-made commodity, available only in small pieces. It was the preserve of the rich and the church, and, as the home-produced product tended to disintegrate, they often imported French glass, cut in quarries (from the French *carré*, a square). These small quarries were fixed into the upper light of the window frame, with shutters or grilles below. More ordinary houses would use only crude wooden shutters, hung to a wood frame. Double shutters, supported by strap hinges, became common during medieval times. The poor used a pattern of reeds, or withies, criss-crossing the open space, and breaking the force of the wind.

Left: Fig. 33 **Shutters and strap-hinges. The photograph is of a rural house but the windows are those of town dwellings four or five hundred years ago. Wooden planks joined together by strap hinges and fastened with a hook.**

Below: Fig. 34 **Parts of the window.**

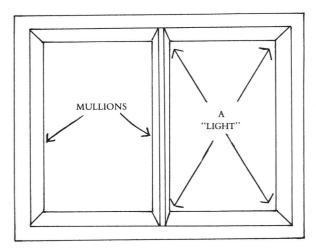

The casement and crown glass

By the sixteenth century, the middle classes were adopting rectangular windows. In wooden-framed houses they would be filled with glass; in fact, Elizabethan buildings used more glass than any other period until the Victorians. In stone houses the window would be divided by stone mullions, for support. Within the sixteenth century, larger house, the spaces would be occupied by hinged, casement windows. Glass was more widely used because of increased home production. The chief type produced was crown glass, which produced particular patterns. The glass was blown from a pipe, and rotated, so that it spread to form a roughly circular sheet. From this were cut small pieces of about 75 square centimetres (12 square inches), recognizable as crown glass by the curving pattern of bubbles within it. Often the pieces were of square or diamond shape and were still called quarries. They were set into lead strips called calms, or cames, and then built into a wooden frame. The square and diamond patterns were often the same as those which had been used to arrange the withies in medieval times. The centre of the sheet, the bullion, was thick and opaque, and was little used. Glass was valued so highly that when someone moved house they often took their windows with them. The poor still relied on shutters and some shopkeepers had begun to use dropping-shutters on chains, designed as a shelf for trading.

Left: Fig. 35   Diamond pattern used in plaiting withies. This arrangement was used for hundreds of years with quarries. *Below left: Fig. 36*   Late-Tudor pattern window in stone, with mullions dividing it into a series of lights. Two casements in the frame and the glass arranged in quarries. Notice also the moulding over the window, called "drip moulding", to carry water away from the frame. *Below: Fig. 37*   Spinning crown glass.

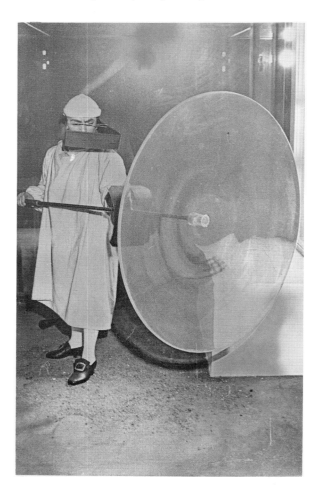

Above: Fig. 38   Yorkshire, or sliding, sash. *Right: Fig. 39*   Half-hung sash above a double-hung sash. Note also the gutters moulded in sandstone and originally lined with lead.

The sash

From 1680, the casement window began to be replaced by the sash window, whose use had spread from the south-west of England. "Sash" comes from the French *chassis*. The window panels slide within a boxed frame, held in position by a system of cords and weights. The first models, "Yorkshire", or sliding sashes, moved horizontally, but almost everywhere they gave way to vertically-opening windows. In the first of this pattern, only one of the two panels moved but, by the end of the seventeenth century, the double-hung sash had appeared, in which both sections could move. This variety is still a common feature in the buildings of the present-day town.

The sash window became widespread in its use for a number of reasons. Technically, it became feasible because larger panels of French glass became available, chiefly from Normandy, although supplies followed from the Newcastle area, first centre of the English trade until the 1840s. These panels, up to 100 square centimetres, were fixed within glazing bars, which divided the window into a series of even sections. This arrangement, which allowed long windows, was suited to the architects and designers of the Renaissance period, and to the arrangement of the windows in the Classical buildings. Tall windows added to the elegance of the style. There was also an increasing passion for fresh air, which the sash window made less uncomfortable. With casements the wind was almost drawn into the room but sashes allowed greater control. The sash style spread throughout the country and, by the middle of the eighteenth century, even small houses had sash windows. The subsequent boom in the demand for glass had one unfortunate side effect. . . .

Window tax and excise duty

From 1695 the Crown levied a tax on glass which continued, with some breaks, until 1845. By that time the tax sometimes amounted to twice the production cost of the glass. Naturally, this restricted the demand for glass and for greater window areas. Window tax, levied on inhabited houses, had an even greater effect. The tax was paid by the occupier on a sliding scale, weighted against those who had many windows in their houses. For example, someone with fifteen windows would pay more than three times the tax as someone with five. The effect of window tax was to restrict the number of windows in houses. Some house-owners bricked up some of their windows to escape the tax although, when this feature is seen, it is not always the result of the tax. Sometimes, it is due to internal rearrangement of the house, or even to a desire to give a symmetry to the exterior, leading to the building of a deliberate dummy window recess. The effect of the window tax was most pronounced in the case of the poor, who could not afford any restriction on the limited light in their houses.

In general, glazed sash windows continued to multiply. Window tax was increased six times between 1746 and 1808, but was halved in 1823 and eventually repealed in 1851. The effect of it, together with excise duty, had been to restrain glass production and to keep its price artificially high. The poor could not afford to replace broken windows, and had to block the holes with paper and rags.

After the repeal of the excise duty, the use of plate glass, which was rolled in larger panels, grew rapidly. It had been produced in St Helens in 1773, but production had remained small. Large panels of "rolled" plate glass were produced by James Hartley in 1847, and, although they needed to be ground and polished before use, the process triggered the large-scale use of glass in all buildings. The Crystal Palace of 1851 ushered in an era when the Victorians used glass in abundance, in conservatories, porches, greenhouses and in a far greater number of windows than had been possible in earlier times. The form of the window did not change much throughout the period, except that they were now set back at least ten centimetres (four inches) in the window space, because of fire regulations. The sash form continued until the early years of the twentieth century. The only changes were simpler glazing bar patterns, a result of the larger panels of glass which could now be afforded.

Modern windows, modern glass

By the beginning of this century, glass was once more, not only a means of allowing light to enter buildings, but an ornamentation. Much late-Victorian glass was engraved, tinted and set in lead, to produce stained-glass windows in many middle-class villas. The Victorians even reproduced the *grisaille* glass of the medieval period, imperfect white glass, painted grey or green, and originally used as quarries in cathedrals. Glass could become more of a decorative

Above: Fig. 40   **Glass buildings. The office block in the rearground is an example of a curtain-walled structure, with glass and aluminium over a steel frame.**

feature because of building improvement. Steel girder frameworks have meant that walls need not bear the whole weight of the building. Increasingly, windows have become a means of decoration and shops and offices have larger and larger areas of glass within them.

After 1900, window forms changed again. Some buildings, and their windows, began to show Elizabethan features. To be correct, the windows had to be casements, first metal, then wood, with the glass arranged in diamond-patterned quarries, held together by strips of lead. The casement remained the dominant pattern almost until the 1950s, with small, transom windows set above. When quarries became too expensive, some houses had strips of lead stuck to the surface of panes to continue the effect of the medieval withies.

From the 1950s onwards, greater areas of glass produced the "picture window", and new processes, such as float glass, introduced in 1958, gave clearer, distortion-free surfaces. In the last twenty years, the British seem to have retreated from the practice of opening all the windows when the weather is fine, and have retired from their fresh-air fetish into an insulated, centrally-heated atmosphere. The function of the window has become more connected with lighting design than ventilation, and the moving and opening parts of the structure are now often of minor importance. In new office buildings, thanks to air-conditioning, windows are not designed to open, the panes are tinted for comfort, and sometimes the whole external surface may be made of glass. Hinges and handles become obsolete in these circumstances, and another stage of development appears, the latest in a long line of adaptations.

6 Regional materials and styles – and their decline

Two hundred years ago, most regions in Britain had their own distinctive buildings which had developed, either through the local abundance of the right materials, or through the special skills of local craftsmen. Materials showed the greatest variation, due to the range of geological outcrops throughout the country. That there has been such regional diversity has been due largely to the fact that, for its size, Britain has a greater variety of rock types than any other country in Europe. The dominant ones range from the beautiful limestones of the Cotswolds, through the sandstones of the Midlands and North-West, to the upland granites and slates. Each of them gives its own quality of colour and scale to buildings. We also have large areas where clays are the surface material, most of them suitable for brick-making and, until two hundred years ago, we could also use our forests of oak, the best-suited of all timbers for the framing of buildings. So, most regions had their own peculiar construction materials, few of which travelled beyond their immediate locality, because of high transport costs.

In upland areas, where trees were scarce, stone had always been the chief material. Walls would be of rubble or dressed stone, depending on the prosperity of the house owner. Roofs would be covered with local flagstone, or a rock like slate which split easily.

In the lowlands, timber and brick were more normal, but

Fig. 41 Dry-stone construction. Many medieval houses would have been built like this in upland areas. Great skill is needed in construction. Notice the use of wood for lintels over the doors.

Fig. 42 Anytown, UK. How would you tell that this was Bristol, rather than Bournemouth or Bolton? The styles seem the same whichever part of the country you visit.

the progressive shortage of good timbers was making their use less common, although they continued to be a minor influence in the south-east into the twentieth century. For the roof, clay tiles would be more likely than flags; thatch was, by this time, being relegated to rural districts. As well as these differences, there were innumerable regional varieties in building design and decoration. Climate was a major influence; in the west and north, the greater rainfall and higher winds made the normal pattern low solid buildings, built of stone. Highland economies were still centred around animals, and the typical hill house was the long-house, part for human use, part for animals. In these areas and their houses, shelter from the weather was of prime importance. The porch, an especially British building feature found in few other countries, served as a shelter for callers and as a place to take off wet clothing and footwear. Window spaces were small, protected by solid shutters and the north and west walls were often thicker and stronger. Sometimes, a special barrier wall was built. By contrast, in the drier, sunnier south and east, construction was less substantial with more decoration on the outside of houses.

Yet, if we look at the larger of our towns, we see little left of this regional variation. In the Central Areas, every "High Street" seems to have been designed by the same architect, using the same limited range of materials. The uniformity of the main shopping areas is even more striking and the effect is reinforced by seeing the same shop signs and names in every part of the country. Look at Figure 42 and spot the similarities between this landscape and that of your nearest large town. The photograph happens to be of Bristol, but it could equally well be twenty other places. There are towns where historic buildings are kept to give a distinct character to the unit, but many are in the process of being cleared because of the mania for producing concrete-and-glass boxes.

Today our buildings are almost part of an international architecture, with close relations in Europe, the Americas, Japan and Australasia. Regional architecture only shows

Left: Fig. 43 Materials before the Transport Revolution. The mis-shaped local brick in the foreground shows the size of the roof slate in the background. It is 80 cm × 45 cm (30 in × 18 in), and weighs more than 6 kilograms (more than 13 lbs). To support this roof, strong timbers were necessary. One of the attractions of the light Welsh slates was their weight, so that builders could save on the cost of timber. *Below: Fig. 44* The porch is a building feature found almost exclusively in Britain, presumably due to the weather. This one shows a bench seat inside, so that callers can take off their wet shoes and boots.

when a particular area is in some way insulated from the property developers. This is true especially of the market and county towns where demand for building land is less intense. One hopeful feature is that the progressive loss of regional building is being halted now, due to preservation and conservation. The decline of regional characteristics dated from the transport improvements, which began in the late eighteenth century. Canals, and later railways, carried building materials to a wider and wider market. Rail was particularly important, and from the middle of the nineteenth century, a growing uniformity resulted. The main beneficiaries of this were the brick and slate industries. Brick replaced stone, because of its speed in construction and the cheap labour involved in its use. The machine-cut Welsh slates produced a new "roofscape" of grey and purple. Before rail improvements, Welsh slate was confined to coastal towns, where there were links by ship to the ports of North Wales.

The nineteenth century saw the rise of the large-scale building contractor. The rapid growth of urban areas often meant that craftsmen were unable to cope with the increased amount of work. They were used to building one house at a time, not street after street. Their skills were not adaptable to rapid work and the introduction of the new materials and the uniformity of the building styles meant that much of the work was repetitive. Building houses all of the same pattern meant that window frames, doors and the roof timbers were of similar size and design whereas previously, individual houses would be tailored, often to fit the dimensions of the main timbers available. Instead of making all the parts on the site, several enterprising builders realized that all the work could be mechanized, on a factory system. The most famous of these were the Cubitt brothers, who built much of London's Belgravia and Pimlico. By the 1820s they had a large factory producing their standardized parts, sending out to their building sites everything from carved-wooden mouldings to wrought-iron railings. In 1851, the Crystal Palace was made of prefabricated parts and assembled by what we would recognize as mass-production methods.

Increasing mechanization and standardization meant a decreasing variety. Craftsmanship declined and, especially in lower-cost housing, speculative builders, erected hectare after hectare of houses, exactly alike. Although it is possible to mourn the loss of local and regional details, there is one advantage in these changes for those studying the urban environment. It has become possible to place and date architectural change, so that periods of town growth can be recognized. Changes in materials within the last hundred and fifty years can be dated quite accurately. Generally, architectural styles have broad bands of time within which they tend to dominate. However, in every case, care is needed when dealing with analyses based on broad generalizations, especially as the introductory dates are usually only relevant in one part of the country, and often only in certain groups of buildings. For example, the pure Georgian form was confined to relatively wealthy occupants, and only traces of the style colour lesser buildings. Nevertheless, a knowledge of such changes is an essential aid for anyone wishing to understand more of their urban environment.

Guide to further study

Bibliography
See the guide to further study, chapter five, page 36, for books on materials and the evolution of housing features. For the development of particular styles, the features of specific periods and the importance of individuals see:

H. Braun, *The Elements of English Architecture* (David & Charles, 1973)

P. W. Kingsford, *Builders and Building Workers* (Arnold, 1973)

H. Pothorn, *Styles of Architecture* (Batsford, 1971)

D. Yarwood, *Outline of English Architecture* (Batsford, 1965)

F. Gibberd, *The Architecture of England from Norman Times to the Present Day* (Architectural Press, 1933)

plus anything from the Pelican History of Art in the Architectural section, especially H. R. Hitchcock's *Architecture. Nineteenth and Twentieth Centuries* (Penguin, 1969).

As a guide to the dating approach

J. T. Smith & E. M. Yates, *On the Dating of English Houses from External Evidence.* (Reprinted from *Field Studies*, vol. II, No. 5, 1968)

Dating surveys, or "age of building" studies, are the most common form of activity connected with the material in this chapter. Information comes both from documentary evidence and from direct observation.

Documentary
Maps: Find when a building/street/area first appears on a map or plan although remember that there is no guarantee that it is the same feature as the one today.

Directories: These are more precise than maps because those from the nineteenth century onward were revised each year.

Local histories: Most towns have their local historian who has dealt with the growth of the area with varying degrees of success. In these local histories areas, at least, will be recorded in terms of their date of construction. Besides the growth of the whole town there are often district histories, written by people like the local vicar or antiquarian. They are not published but duplicated and if they exist will be found in branch libraries which usually have a file of material on local, i.e. district, history.

Archives: Some main libraries will have records such as title deeds, particularly for larger houses or in districts where the local corporation is or was a major landowner. Many urban developments have been at the expense of private estates and the records of these estates and the sale of their land may be in archive sections.

Local authority material: Much twentieth century building has been carried out by local authorities and they will have records and plans of their constructions.

Newspapers: Libraries and newspaper record rooms may be a source of information but only if you already have a general idea of the date.

Observation
Beside the broad outline given by architectural style there are other guides, of varying degrees of reliability.

Date plaques: Many buildings of the nineteenth century had stone or plaster records of their date of building, usually in a prominent place on upper floors. They are usually a reliable source of information on that building, but not necessarily on those around it. Look also for dates on the boxes of gutter down-spouts. These are quite frequent on eighteenth-century "grand" buildings but also appear on revivalist buildings of the twentieth century.

Street names and district names: Very frequently streets and districts about to be built up were named after events or individuals famous in that particular period and this can act as a general guide in dating. See the guide to further study for chapter twelve for further references.

There are of course many other exercises which can be carried out using information of this type. Bricks or other materials can be recorded and measured to see how they change according to their period of use. Graphing the use of particular materials can produce interesting studies which may interrelate with transport work, e.g. did the coming of the railway produce a change in roofing from flags to slate. Again refer to the books on methods and techniques at the end of chapter eleven.

Study 4 Dating by style

Methods of approach

Tables IV and V show some of the ways in which the study of buildings and streets can be approached. It is possible to begin with a simple approach and progressively to isolate the individual factors in any landscape feature. Each stage in the study brings an increase in the amount of detail. For example, in studying buildings we could follow the branch dealing with material, concentrate on walls and examine the different elements which might be used. The brick example is taken a stage further, showing how a more detailed study might be organized and this could be extended to increasingly intensive aspects. While description of the characteristics is useful in itself, the main point of the classification is to enable explanation of the features from a mainly historical viewpoint.

(a) *Walls and walling*

Over the last five hundred years almost every facet of the urban landscape has undergone change in terms of its material, style and organization. Very few have retained any of their original characteristics. Table VI on page 46 summarizes the main trends which have taken place in buildings and their development. Very few of the columns show any continuity. The features which have appeared over the longest period are the obvious ones such as stone as a building material. Mud is another one. It surprises many people to learn that mud was still used until the 1920s, under its regional name of cob. Some of the features disappeared and returned, as fashion, or techniques, changed. It is beyond the scope of this book to explain all the complex reasons for the change and development of

Some approaches to the analysis of town features. The sub-divisions could be extended very easily. *Below:* Table V   Paths and streets. *Left:* Table IV   Buildings.

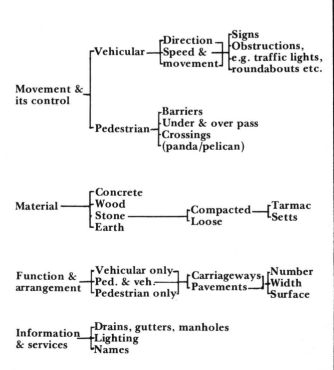

Style & characteristics
- Wall features
  - Doors and entrances
  - Decorative additions
  - Windows
- Roof features
  - Gutters
  - Pitch
  - Decoration
  - Style
  - Chimneys
- Dimensions

Surface material
- Roof
  - Slate
  - Concrete
  - Tile → Concrete / Clay
  - Thatch and wood
  - Stone
  - Others
- Wall
  - Timber
  - Concrete
  - Rendered
  - Tile
  - Brick → Colour / Size / Bond / Arrangement & pattern
  - Stone
  - Others

Organization
- Multiple
  - Terrace
  - Intermediate
  - High-rise
- Duplex (semi-detached)
- Single (detached)

Function
- Residential
- Retail & commercial
- Public

Movement & its control
- Vehicular
  - Direction
  - Speed & movement → Signs / Obstructions, e.g. traffic lights, roundabouts etc.
- Pedestrian
  - Barriers
  - Under & over pass
  - Crossings (panda/pelican)

Material
- Concrete
- Wood
- Stone → Compacted → Tarmac / Setts / Loose
- Earth

Function & arrangement
- Vehicular only
- Ped. & veh.
- Pedestrian only → Carriageways / Pavements → Number / Width / Surface

Information & services
- Drains, gutters, manholes
- Lighting
- Names

Table VI   Aids to the dating of urban details. These are only guidelines and they should not be taken as precise limits in any area

	BRICK										WOOD	OTHERS	RENDERED FINISHES
		COMMON SIZES IN USE						BONDING	PATTERNS	COLOUR			
		Inches			Millimetres								
Medieval (up to 1485)	C13 The term "brick" comes into use from C15, replacing the term "waltyle"	5½	3¾	1½	140	66	38	English & irregular bonding. Wide mortar courses because of variation in individual brick size.	Red and plum	Patterns from France in C15	Dominant material in common houses. Use as part of frame and as shingles	Rubble stone & freestone. Masonry only on large houses	Cob; Wattle & daub; Limewashing poor timbers; Pargetting
	C15 Dutch Tudor	6–8½ / 10¼–12½	3–3¾ / 5–6	1⅜–1¾ / 1¾–2¾	152–216 / 261–318	76–95 / 127–152	35–44 / 44–70						
1485–1600	C16 1571 Statute brick (regulated size)	9	4½	2¼	228	114	57		Red Orange; Use of blue in headers	Diamonds Diaper-work Brick nogging – herringbone	Decline in competition with brick because of fire hazard	Decrease in use because of high labour costs in masonry. Stone in quoins only	Rough-cast; Pebble dash
1600–1800	C17 1625	9	4½	3	228	114	76	English garden wall; Flemish	Chequering & diaper. Most depends on contrasts between stretchers & headers in Flemish bond			Artificial stones; Use of weather tiles & "brick tiles" because of brick tax dies out 1850	Stucco duro; Ornamental pargetting
	C18 From 1784 brick tax increases size	9	4½	3–3¼	228	108	76–82				1774 London Building Act virtually prohibits use		
Nineteenth Century	C19 large bricks taxed more heavily	8¾	4 3/16	2⅝–2⅞	222	106	67–72		Mid Victorian "strong" colours; Light sand-lime bricks	Some use as weather-boarding after brick tax; Use in gables and in Tudor	Last period of widespread use before cheap transport allows brick to become dominant	1830s: first concretes; 1867: reinforced concrete; 1880: pre-stressed concrete	Stucco out by 1850
	End of brick tax	8¼–9	3⅞–4¼	1½–3	210–230	100–110	38–75						
Twentieth Century	Most common modern size	8½	4	2½	215	102.5	65	Stretcher (cavity walls)	Wider variety of decorative colours	Tudor revival Brick nogging patterns	revival half-timbered exteriors; Cedar wood as external cladding	Coloured reconstituted stone; Use of concrete in high-rise buildings; Increased use in wider variety of forms	Pebble dash; Widespread covering of concrete & breeze block by plaster & cement rendering

	ROOF FEATURES			WINDOWS	DOORS	OTHER DETAILS	HOUSE STYLES IN TOWNS
	MATERIAL	STYLE	CHIMNEYS & GUTTERS				
Medieval (up to 1485)	Stone tiles since Roman period; Natural frost-shattered sheets laid with heaviest at base of roof	Often multi-gabled, facing onto streets	Chimneys begin in C11 often acting as central support for upper-storey timbers; Gutters used, even in thatched roofs – but no down spouts	Window spaces filled with glass only in richer houses – glass in small pieces, set in lead. Most houses have wooden shutters on pin or strap hinges. Spaces long & divided by mullions – or small & square	Planks or battens on strap hinges	Jettying the only way to produce tall buildings	Terraces of wood or wood & stone; Large houses detached; Few more than two storeys high
1485–1600	Clay tiles on small houses; Decorated "cox comb" ridge tiles; Slates and flags; Pantiles from low countries fashionable until 1900		Tall decorated Tudor chimneys in moulded bricks; Large houses have box gutter in lead – water drains through gaps or gargoyles	Poor use reeds plaited in diamond pattern. Windows taller, divided into series of lights. High-income housing uses casements, with quarries set in lead			Courtyards develop as towns increase in population
1600–1800	Lead used on neo-Classical flattish roofs	Low-angle roofs of neo-Classical style	Central chimney stack disappears. Stack to side of larger houses. Gutters under eaves – square lead or cast-iron in large houses, V-shaped wooden in small	Windows in neo-Classical buildings tall & arranged symmetrically. Casements replaced by sashes from 1680. Larger panels of glass but windows restricted by window tax & excise duty	Door becomes central part of renaissance design. Queen Anne doors with hood and fanlight to give light to hall. Georgian: no hood	Wrought-iron work balconies & railings with fine details. The central kennel begins to be replaced by side gutters – down spouts become common	Neo-Classical houses, regular, single or terrace, symmetrical proportions. Back-to-backs appear
Nineteenth Century	Beginnings of slate transport from 1820; Slate roofs with decoration (finial & cresting tiles); 1882: end of tax on tiles	Change of pitch with lighter Welsh slates – high angle roofs with steep gables & belvederes; Hipped roofs with	Cast-iron gutters. Large houses have tall chimneys with numerous pots. Semi-circular iron gutters	Window tax & excise duty ended. Glass prices fall and increased window space possible in all houses. Sash remains chief pattern	– replaced by Classical pediment. Mass production of doors gives standard pattern of panelled door. Victorians use glass as decoration in panels & side lights of porch – copies,	Wrought-iron work changes to cast – much heavier. Mass-produced mechanized wood-carving as decoration on all houses. Verandahs & greenhouses	Victorian villas, large for increased families; Courts back to back; Industrial terraces & tenements
Twentieth Century	Concrete tiles from c.1907; Flat roofs in concrete; Corrugated iron, timber & felt roofs	gables; some complicated Alpine patterns; Simple hipped roofs for houses – post 1945 due to high cost of construction; Large buildings with flat concrete roofs	Tudor revival brings tall chimneys; Chimney begins to disappear because of central heating; Plastic guttering	Casement reappears – small quarries also; Picture window with transoms the only moving section	medieval stained glass; Use of coloured glass continues to 1930s; Tudor door returns – planks with metal studs; Clear glass panelled doors, fully glazed	Garages	The semi-detached local authority & private estate development; High-rise maisonettes

each individual characteristic. Here we can only mention the main trends.

Traditional walling materials are stone and wood. Although wood has ceased to be a widespread feature of towns, stone is till widely visible. Traditional stone building is often of rubble stone with dressed stone, or masonry, appearing only in important structures. Most stone buildings which we see now are of masonry, as the rubble stone has been demolished, or covered with rendering. Bricks, originally large, thin and known as "waltyles", became more important from the sixteenth century onwards, but their development was restricted by the brick tax, which lasted from 1784 until 1850. The tax, paid on the number of bricks made, encouraged the production of larger bricks. It also gave a greater incentive to use other materials, such as wood, which reappeared as weather-boarding, planks nailed to the wall, or brick tiles, half an inch thick. All materials have a decorative element, either because of their colour, or the patterns in which they are arranged. Brickwork has, for hundreds of years, been bonded in different-coloured bands, diamonds or chequerwork. Less attractive materials, however, need to be decorated, and so we have rendering, finishes applied to brick and stone. They are probably more common now than ever before, because we use materials with plainly unattractive surfaces, such as breeze-blocks and concrete, and so we cover them with painted plaster. Medieval houses used a mixture of lime and sand, mixed with cow hair as an external wall covering. Later, exotic elements were added, such as cheese, beer, cow dung, bullocks' blood and barley water. Later still, rendered "stucco" finishes became characteristic of Queen Anne and Regency buildings. After this a period of a hundred years passes before the pebble-dashed walls of the 1920s and 30s.

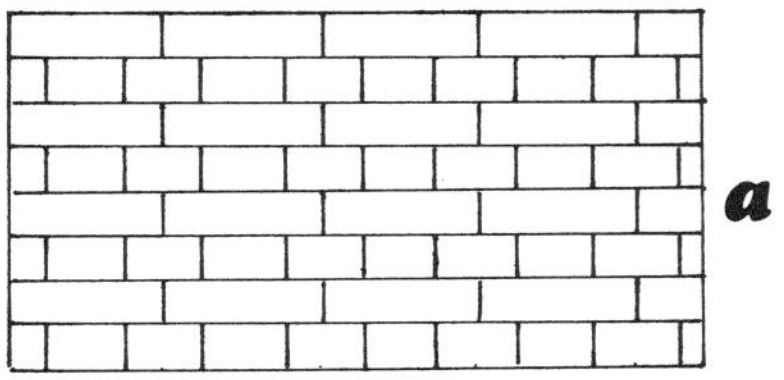

Fig. 45 Types of brick bonding and patterns (a) English bond. Alternate courses of headers and stretchers; (b) English garden-wall bond. Either three or five courses of stretchers to one of headers; (c) Flemish bond. Alternate headers and stretchers in each course; (d) Flemish garden-wall bond. Three stretchers to one header in each course; (e) Header bond; (f) Soldier bond. Used mainly in single courses, as on tops of party walls; (g) Stretcher bond. A modern arrangement, used as a double-(cavity)wall, in recent buildings; (h) Chequer-work patterns; (j) Diaper (diamond) patterns.

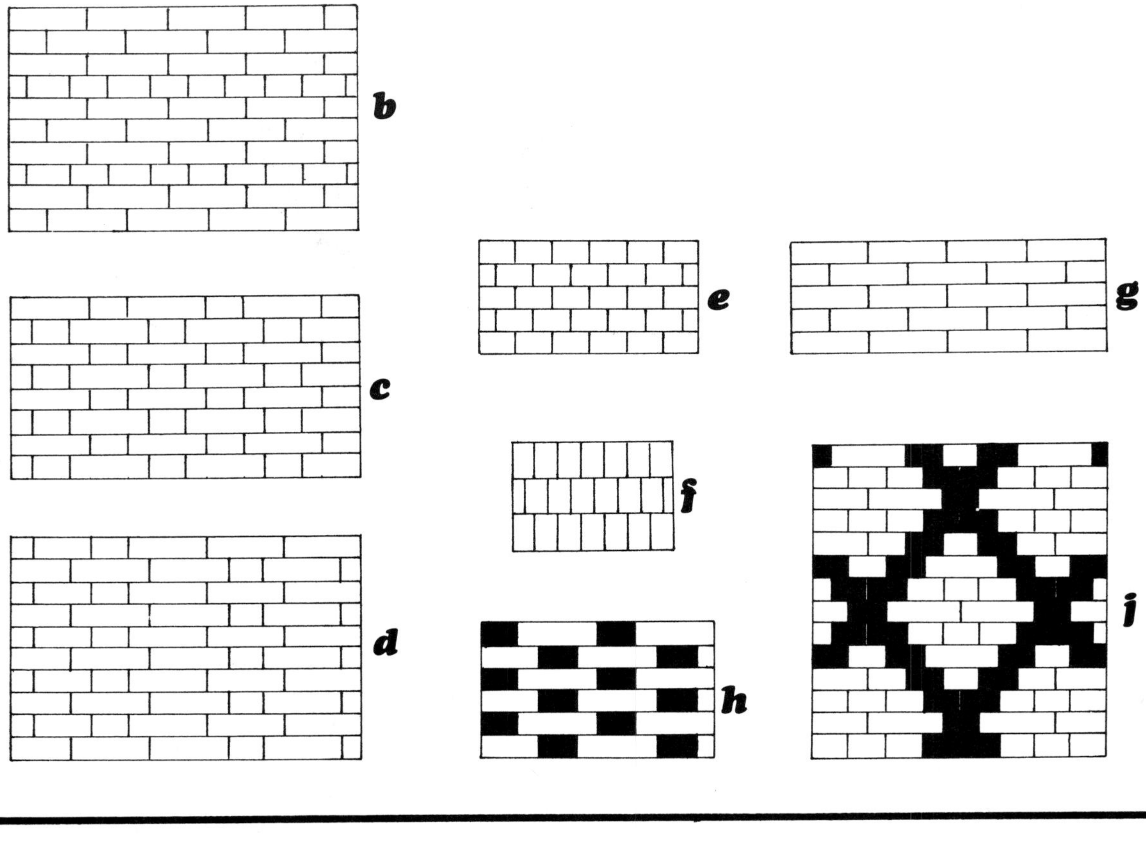

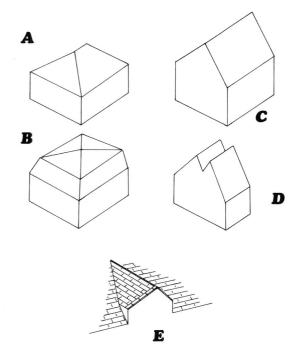

(b) *Roofs and roof styles*

Roofs also have a complex history. They begin with a framework of branches, covered with turf, and develop slowly into a detailed arrangement of load-bearing roof timbers. British roofs have one main purpose: to keep out rain. They also have to shed the water which falls on them. So they should not only be made of the most convenient impermeable material, but also be built so that the water drains away. The differences in material, the angles of slope, the gutters and spouts, are features which have varied throughout time. The style of the roof has also changed, both because of the desire to use the attic space and because roofs are sometimes designed for attraction and appeal or as part of an overall plan, as in the low-angle Georgian style. In our towns and cities we see mainly the modern roofs. The older materials, wood, thatch and thick stone flags, have largely disappeared. Lead remains in some cases, as it has a life-span of some three hundred years, but the major materials are slate and tile. Slate was the great roofing material of the nineteenth century, most of it coming from the Welsh quarries as new canals and railways gave it cheaper transport. Some idea of the importance of these improvements to the slate industry can be gained from the statistics of the cost of transport as a percentage of the eventual selling price of slate. In 1790, the cost of carrying slate from Caernarvon to London formed sixty-one per cent

Above: Fig. 47   Roof styles. There are two basic forms of roof, the hipped roof which recedes from the line of the wall, and the gabled roof which continues the line of the wall. The diagrams above give some examples of the variations: (A) simple hipped roof; (B) nipped Mansard roof, named after the Frenchman François Mansart (1598–1666) who first designed it; (C) simple gabled roof; (D) gabled "W-shaped" roof; (E) gable built from the roof-line to form a "dormer" feature.

Right: Fig. 48   Neo-Classical door. The style belongs only to this period and is a good example of how individual features can be used for dating.

Below: Fig. 46   Slate patterns. The early slates were heavy and were laid so that the smallest were at the apex of the roof and the heaviest were near the eaves. When the smaller, lighter Welsh varieties arrived, more regular patterns resulted. (A) the old arrangement, (B) the more recent one.

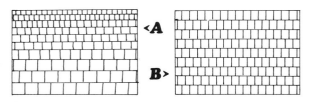

of the total cost; a hundred years later, it was twelve per cent. Another factor leading to the increase in the use of the light, Welsh slates, was the lack of home-grown timber, and the increasing cost of imported varieties. Light slates only needed a thin supporting framework. By the beginning of this century, the influence of slate was on the wane and the introduction of the cement tile, from 1906 onwards, brought a competitor which was to seal its fate.

Simple hipped and gabled roofs are the most common variation we see but the Victorians provided variety with their dormer rooms within the attics, each gabled and decorated. Many modern houses show the same design, using the space in the roof for new bedrooms, or play areas.

This study does not attempt a full review of all building features and styles, but only tries to introduce the most important ones. Because many of the terms used may be new to the reader, a glossary of the more unusual ones is given below.

Simple glossary of building terms

Ashlar   Dressed stones as a facing for walls. The interior could be of irregular material.

Belvedere   A turret projecting from the roof line.

Bond   The arrangement of individual bricks within a wall. See page 47.

Box gutter   One which is square in shape.

Breeze block   A building material formed under compression of ash, or clinker, mixed with cement.

Brick nogging   The in-filling by brick of the spaces between the timbers in a framed house. It often replaced plaster and was usually in a herringbone pattern.

Cavity wall   One with a continuous gap between the outer and inner sections. It uses *stretcher bond* and is a feature of modern housing.

Chequerwork   Alternate *headers* and *stretchers* of different colours. See page 47.

Classical (or neo-Classical) features   Architectural details copied from the Classical orders. For names and relationships, see pages 52, 53.

Cladding   A general term for the covering of surfaces, especially by wood or tile.

Cob   A mixture of raw clay and straw.

Cresting tile   One in a series crowning the ridge of a roof. Medieval and neo-Gothic patterns were ornamental; modern ones are semi-circular and of cement.

Diaper   A diamond-shaped pattern in a wall. In brickwork it is obtained by using different coloured bricks. See page 47.

Dormer   A window in an upper floor, built outward from the roof line.

Dressed stone   Smoothly-finished stonework. Also called masonry.

Finial tile   Ornamental feature at the top of turrets, or the point of gables. Used especially in Victorian or Edwardian neo-Gothic building.

Freestone   A stone which splits along regular divisions and which can be used for laying continuous courses.

Gable   The triangular section beneath a ridged roof. See pages 48, 49.

Gargoyle   A decorated spout carrying rain water away from the wall.

Gothic   A style of architecture best developed in the late Middle Ages, especially in churches. Its main feature is the pointed arch.

Half timbering   The technique in timber framing which uses halved timbers as opposed to whole logs.

Header   The smallest section of a standard brick.

Herringbone pattern   An arrangement in brickwork, dating from Tudor times, where courses were laid to form a zigzag pattern.

Hipped roof   See roof diagrams on page 48.

Jettying   The projection of the upper floors in timber-framed buildings. See page 63.

Kennel   A central gutter common in courts and older streets.

Mansard roof   See roof diagrams on page 48.

Mullion   A vertical division within a window space.

Pantile   A roof tile with an S-shaped profile.

Pargetting (or parging)   Decoration in plaster. Often used for the panels between the timbers of framed houses.

Pebble dash   A type of wall covering formed by planting small stones in the rendering while it is still wet.

Quoin   A corner stone of a building.

Reinforced concrete   Slabs or beams of concrete with steel reinforcing bars set within them.

Rendering   The covering of the load-bearing structure by plasters and cement.

Shingle   A flat wooden tile, originally of oak, used especially in early churches.

Speculative builder   One who buys land and builds without having a guaranteed customer.

Stretcher   The longest side in a standard brick.

Stucco   A *rendering* of lime, gypsum or cement, used particularly in the late eighteenth and nineteenth centuries to cover brickwork, or poor stone.

Terracotta   "Cooked earth". Fine clay, mixed with sand, and fired to great hardness. Usually moulded into decorative shapes.

Transom   A horizontal glazing bar in a window frame. Now used for the small rectangular window at the top of modern frames.

Wattle and daub   A mixture of lime and sand, mixed with cow or ox hair and used on external surfaces.

Weather boarding   Wood planks, tongued and grooved. An external wall covering used mainly in the south-east of England.

7 Eccentricities

Above: Fig. 50 **Late-Victorian decorative ironwork – an expensive whim of the architect, with no practical function.**

There was a word of caution given before the last study about the need for care in using a series of generalized tables. Luckily, our towns and cities are not made up entirely of standardized, interchangeable units. Most towns are fortunate in having individual buildings, or groups, which belong to no particular style, or to a combination of styles, and which are the creations of non-conforming individuals. Our surroundings would lose much of their appeal without the influence of eccentricity and personal whim.

Most people have at some time passed through areas, such as large housing estates, where the only differences between the buildings may be the colour of the curtains, or the height of the hedge. There is no apparent individuality, although the occupants may have widely differing personalities and tastes. Yet, in the middle of such areas, one often finds an oddity, something which stands out from the uniformity around it. It might be a Victorian Gothic castle, guarded by battlements and turrets, complete with arrow slits. Or perhaps a Swiss *chalet*, transported from the Alps. Whatever it is, the presence of such diversions makes the material in the last study a series of guidelines, tendencies rather than laws. The variations possible in any one aspect of buildings and their details are enormous, and in many ways it makes it very difficult to define the characteristics of the "normal" pattern. The differences which we see around us are often the result of the personal attitudes and wishes of the architect, the owner or the user, and we cannot ignore their influence upon the urban environment.

Such individual decision took wider reign in the past than it does at present. There are now many forms of restriction on the individual to build what he likes. Most of these are the social controls for which we use the term planning, which have become powerful relatively recently. Two hundred years ago the only obstacle to indulging oneself with a "Roman" temple or a "Crusader's" castle was finance. The rich were able to build on a large scale, while the poor were confined to minute detail. Increasingly, restrictions have meant that even the rich are somewhat more sober in their outbursts of eccentricity. This is not to say that idiosyncrasy has ceased to operate as a theme in our urban environment. There may not be the same number of "sham" castles and palaces built as there were in Victorian times, but the copying of past styles has become a trend more associated with lower-cost building. In the following study, we examine some of the cycles in building style and taste which help to provide some of the diversity in our surroundings.

Guide to further study

The architectural books in the study guide for chapter six give more detail on the features associated with "revivalist" styles. Most of the variations outlined in this section should be fairly obvious after some preliminary reading.

After having recognized them, the question arises, what do we do with the information? Placing them on the historical stage is one answer. Another might be to give points for the number of features which differ from the "norm", whatever might be thought to be the ordinary house of the area. In this way variations in housing style could be mapped.

Another way of looking at the features of the built environment comes more into the field of landscape and design. This is the "townscape" approach and useful books include

K. Lindley, *Townlook Book 2* (Pergamon, 1970)
T. Sharp, *Town and Townscape* (Murray, 1968)
E. Johns, *British Townscapes* (Arnold, 1965)
G. Cullen, *Townscape* (Architectural Press, 1971)

Left: Fig. 49 **A real original. This sort of feature defies explanation, except if it is viewed as the idea of someone with very definite and individual wishes. Black and white does not do justice to its attraction, as it is built up of coloured tiles. The design seems to have been strongly influenced by Turkish architecture, but it really belongs to no style but its own.**

Study 5 Revivals and follies

The Gothic Revival

In 1819, Sir Walter Scott (1771–1832) published the first of his great, English historical novels, *Ivanhoe*, and it was to be followed by others with titles such as *Tales of the Crusaders*. Whether Scott led the fashion for returning to the delights of medieval life, or whether he followed it, his books coincided with an outbreak of mock-castle building in Britain. Looking backwards to the time of the Black Knight and Sir Brian de Bois-Guilbert, they often appeared as replicas of early medieval structures, complete with draw-bridges and arrow slits. One of the more notable of these "follies" had the following text inscribed upon it: "I have raised up the ruins, and builded it as in days of old". These buildings were some of the more lunatic examples of the beginning of the "Gothic Revival", which overwhelmed Britain in the nineteenth century.

In the eighteenth, the main architectural influence had been what was called neo-(new)Classical; famous architects, such as Nash, Hawksmoor and the Woods, built according to the traditions of ancient Greece and Rome. The movement had been established in Britain since the work of Inigo Jones in the seventeenth century. The rebuilding of St Paul's, which began in 1675, marks the beginning of the English Classical style, with the purer Greek and Roman influences becoming stronger after 1730.

By the start of the nineteenth century, neo-Classical details embroidered most buildings of any importance. The influence of the style continued throughout the rest of the century, but was increasingly challenged by the neo-Gothic. The story of their rivalry for supremacy explains the features of most of our remaining Victorian buildings.

The neo-Classical period took place in Britain at the same time as our most extravagant era of social life, at least for the affluent. During the seventeenth and eighteenth centuries, fashionable town life was characterized by the dandy, the club and by a liberal attitude towards sexual escapades. The buildings often reflected this way of life, extravagant, elegant and with a grace and symmetry we have not seen since. The Victorian period saw a reaction against this life-style, *and* its architecture. The Gothic style which replaced it was seen as, not merely an architectural change, but as an expression of a different morality. Whereas, in the Georgian period, the Gothic was viewed as a Romantic form, and Classical forms stood for Reason, the Victorians gave the styles a religious overtone. The Gothic stood for

Below left: Fig. 51   **The main characteristics of the Classical style.** *Below: Fig. 52*   **A beautiful set of offices. Such a title would be very difficult to give to many of today's buildings, but this nineteenth-century structure is of a different breed, designed with an eye to attraction as well as economy.**

Christianity, the Classical for Paganism. With the Victorians' public enthusiasm for Christianity, the Gothic form began to triumph.

Churches are one obvious area in which we can see a relatively pure form of Gothic Revival. Here were reproduced the buttresses and arched windows of the medieval cathedrals. However, it also had a pronounced effect upon all other buildings of the time. Towers, spires, turrets and battlements grew in profusion on Victorian villas. Many were ugly, huge expanses of polychrome brick, red, brown and yellow, crowned by steep pinnacles of slate. Figure 53 shows an example of a Victorian folly, with a tower *and* a turret, serving an unknown purpose. Most of our towns and cities have good examples of this type, often converted into flats or some form of hotel or hostel. They are the dinosaurs of the built environment, their style and their size making them difficult to integrate into our present pattern. In the Central Areas of our urban districts, neo-Gothic appears widely, marking the great economic expansion of Victorian Britain. Town halls and insurance offices rise like cathedrals, mirrors of the pride and ambition of the period. The same is true of the Classical buildings in our urban units, except that the ones which remain often have more beauty and balance than the Gothic.

Other revivals and new influences

Middle and low-cost building absorbed much from the Gothic movement. Doorways, window shapes, roof styles were copied and added onto the conventional terrace form. The influence continued until the beginning of the First World War, when new forms of fancy appeared. A revival of Tudor building saw a timber frame built onto the brickwork. Reproduction gables would be black and white, with plasterwork replacing wattle-and-daub. Sometimes brick would be the in-filling arranged in herringbone pattern, as in medieval brick nogging. Figure 54 shows a house front with these features, complete with quarry pattern windows and even a reproduction of a medieval cast, down spout. In the 1920s comes a time of Mediterranean influence. Suburban villas were rendered and painted white; perhaps the warm summers of this period convinced builders that climatic change was ahead. Some of the houses had flat roofs, poorly adapted to our wet climate. Others used pantiles, copying the roofscape of Italian villages. Swiss *chalets* were another variety which had a temporary vogue, along with Spanish *haciendas*.

For the first time in hundreds of years, large numbers of one-storeyed houses were built. The bungalow, a name of Hindu origin, was the legacy of colonial India, brought back, along with the verandah, a feature necessary in tropical climates. Totally unsuited to our weather, the verandah soon disappeared, but the bungalow remains with

Below: Fig. 53   **Calling the faithful to prayer? Grafted on to a large but fairly normal Victorian house are an entrance area, with a porch large enough for a baronial hall, a tower, the upper part of which seems to serve no purpose except perhaps a last retreat if the house were attacked and a spire and turret suitable for imprisoned maidens to shout from, or Islamic muezzins to call to local believers!** *Below right: Fig. 54*   **The Tudor revival (see text above).**

us, still a popular housing style. Our present time is marked by an epidemic of "neo-Georgian" construction. Most of this seems just to involve placing a bow window within an otherwise nondescript exterior. The revival has none of the style of the original, but this is really to be expected. Very few of the reconstructions of the last hundred and fifty years have had the appeal of the original model, and many remain as objects of amusement. Nevertheless, they were the dream and pride of people in the past, reflections of ideas and attitudes of their period, and therefore important as expressions of their time. Also, they do serve the very valuable purpose of enlivening what is becoming an increasingly uniform urban environment.

Below: Fig. 54 **Tudor and Indian influences. Early twentieth century with a verandah open to the weather and used only by the hardiest of the occupants. The verandah roof is of "fish-scale" slates, with a half-round face, popular as a form of decoration. The upper storey is imitation half-timbered with machine-cut uprights and curved braces, bolted to the brickwork beneath and the spaces filled with plaster, painted white.**

8 Social use and social value

If economic and technical factors were the only ones causing the features of our urban areas, then we should have far less variation than we have today. Follies do, after all, represent a very small proportion of our building stock. However, the style, size and function of our buildings and the use of the remainder of the area respond to other factors, which we may call "social use" and "social value". To give an example, churches are a common feature of every urban area. They often occupy prime building land, sometimes in commercially very desirable areas, presumably having outbidden other potential users for the site, but they have no commercial justification. They are often built in ornate styles, costing far more than would a simple structure which could fulfil the same purpose. Someone had to put up the money to pay for the site and construction. Yet, having been built, it gives back no rent or other profit. It makes no money for anyone. Purely economic arguments could not account for its existence. It is only possible to explain churches as a feature in our environment by introducing the fact that most societies are religious, having a set of beliefs which sometimes need buildings or areas for their ceremonies. If society had no such beliefs or attitudes, then there would be no churches. In the same way, an increasing proportion of our urbanized areas is given over to public parks and recreation fields. Their growth within towns dates only from the middle of the nineteenth century and marks a change in the views of society in general, and local and national government in particular. People began to recognize a need for public open space, especially for the inhabitants of the courts and terraces. Social use and value, in the context of this book, involves a number of approaches, each of which is mainly concerned with the attitude of groups of people or with the behaviour of the whole of the population.

For example, when we looked at the development of low-income housing, it was possible to see that the attitudes of people in authority changed during the period under consideration. In the early and mid-nineteenth century, with the exception of a liberal few, upper-class opinion clearly stated that the housing conditions of the poor were due to the poor themselves. If they were placed in more agreeable houses, they would rapidly produce the same conditions as before, because their natural way of life was one of filth and squalor. In more recent times, a common argument against putting baths into council houses was that people would use them for keeping the coal in. Throughout the last hundred and fifty years, progress in local authority housing has been related to a gradual change in the views of those in authority, a realization that people's habits *could* be changed by improving their environment.

Land economics gave us a theoretical zonation of urban areas, in which the centre was the most desirable location. The use of this Central Area becomes concentrated into the fields of commerce and specialized retail outlets, but even here the idea of social value can be seen. If one examines the styles of the buildings in the centre, particularly those of the nineteenth and early twentieth centuries, their imposing size and ornamentation is striking. Very often the public buildings of the time, the town halls, museums and art galleries were built on monumental lines. Whether Gothic or Classical, they were of huge size, particularly in the larger industrial towns. Sometimes they were consciously ostentatious, built to glorify the power and strength of the growing towns and councils. Neighbouring towns would attempt to outdo each other in building the largest and most expensive features. The results could be said to be the effects of a social attitude – civic pride. In the same way commercial institutions, such as banks and insurance offices seemed to equate size with dependability. Banks were very keen to give the impression of security and, even in suburban areas, they were built like small fortresses. Today the functions of the centre are still determined by ideas of status as well as convenience. There are, in every town, examples of streets which are associated with certain trades or professions, which see the particular address as giving them respectability. Harley Street is one of the most famous of these, but every large town has its specialized areas. If one is to understand the patterns in the urban unit, it is important to recognize that area status is in some cases as important as accessibility and other economic criteria.

The same response can be seen in housing. When, in the nineteenth century, the rich moved out from the centre of the town, they chose their new area carefully. They were moving from the smell of the tanneries and the glue factories, or from the fear of infection, or from contact with the dirty and diseased, and they made their decisions so that links with the town would be minimized. In Britain, it was supposed to be a natural part of the pattern that the rich were to be found in the south-western quadrant of the urban area. The reasons for this were mainly climatic. The prevailing wind, blowing normally from the south-west, would blow smoke and smells toward the north and east. This is not true everywhere in Britain for, on the east coast, a seasonal easterly wind could cause the reverse. Whatever the direction, the process did lead to certain locations being favoured by the rich and acquiring a social status. In 1662, it

Left: Fig. 55 **The nineteenth-century school and its surroundings. Typical of arrangements within the industrial towns and cities, this shows the lack of playing space, both for the school and within the environment.**

was commented that London was growing westward to escape the "fumes, steams and stinks of the great easterly pyle". The whole feature might be called the West End mentality, as it is best seen in social attitudes towards housing within London. In all cases, sections of the town acquire a particular status long after the original factors, smells and smoke, have diminished. The social allegiances to these areas continue today, and an address in these high-status districts is a mark of distinction, although presumably the house could be shared by a dozen families. Conversely, some districts are associated with low-order housing, what the Americans call "living on the wrong side of the tracks". This type of social impression can play a big part in shaping the patterns of buildings and land use in towns and cities.

Amenity land – parks, gardens and recreation space – are nowadays found more and more in the area around the perimeter of our towns and cities, where the most recent developments have taken place. In the town centres, there is a smaller proportion of amenity land to building land, unless you are fortunate, as in London, to have former royal estates or, as in Southampton, the remains of common lands. Members of early nineteenth-century authorities saw little need to give over valuable land to such diversions, especially as they had their own extensive private gardens. The first public parks in Britain did not appear until the 1830s, with the opening of the Victoria Park in Bath. The first large parks were Princes in Liverpool, opened 1842, and Birkenhead Park, opened 1844. Both were designed by Joseph Paxton (1801–65) who designed the building which was later re-erected as the Crystal Palace. They were the forerunners of many more, often bought out of public subscription gathered, curiously enough, mainly from the rich. What brought about this change in attitude among the affluent? As more and more poor people crowded into the growing towns, so the statistics showed a sharp rise in crime. The Victorian upper-classes were naturally concerned for themselves and their property. Gardens were locked and barred, spiked railings ceased to be decorations and private parks with gatehouses and keepers became common for protection against footpads and beggars. Public parks were seen as a way of improving the morality of the poor; instead of plotting criminal deeds in their rooms, they could commune with Nature and let the fresh air drive out their impure thoughts. There was also the growing fad for sunshine and fresh air as cures for illness. Much of the improvement brought about in the Public Health Acts was made acceptable to the middle- and upper-classes by associating the progress with the fight against vice and crime.

Schools are another area where enormous differences can be seen between they physical organization of Victorian buildings and those we have today. The nineteenth-century Board school had a cramped, flagged playground, and organized games were limited. Modern schools, surrounded by their own playing fields, are a marked contrast. Changes such as these have come slowly, as the standards previously enjoyed by the privileged have only gradually spread to the majority.

Guide to further study

Some of the suggestions arising from this section come under the term "perception". Here it may be interesting to find and compare people's views on where the "better" areas of the town are, where they consider the most desirable zone to be. Is there a West End mentality in the town, even if it does not relate to that particular direction? Also try plotting the location of specialist professions from the Yellow Pages directories. Do they cluster around particular zones? It is possible to measure the degrees of concentration on a relative scale (see the study guide to chapter eleven). Medical specialists and barristers/solicitors are good examples to start with.

The growth of publicly-owned social facilities can be studied from maps and records. Directories and local histories will give dates when baths, parks and schools opened. One way of comparing past and present attitudes to leisure and recreation is to measure the percentages of the built-up area devoted to parks, gardens and playing fields. This can be done quite easily by producing a fine grid on tracing paper, placing it onto town maps of various historical periods, and estimating percentages of the total area under specific uses by counting squares. This method of quadrat analysis can be very useful for a variety of studies.

Population statistics for the local area can be obtained from the Census but the smallest unit is the census district. Individual information is most complete in parish registers which may be in the possession of the individual church or in the Record Office. One of the most fascinating ways of studying changes in patterns of mortality and life expectancy is within graveyards. Graves are a mine of information on such factors as place of birth, and with it migration, age at death (see the large number of young children in early times) and occupations. Remember though that the poor often could afford no headstone and their lives and deaths are largely unrecorded. For further information see

K. Lindley, *Graves and Graveyards* (Routledge & Kegan Paul, 1972)

One of the best sources of statistics is the Government publication *Social Trends* mentioned at the end of chapter two. This now appears every year and for population gives details of total population, age and sex structure, family size and expectation of life. Most of these statistics are for the Census dates within this century, i.e. 1901–71, and are a useful record of change.

Study 6 Family size and the need for housing

Living together, or living apart

Changes in the size and organization of the family have had an enormous influence upon the urban landscape. Such changes bring different social attitudes towards types of homes and styles of living. The most famous of these attitudes is "an Englishman's home is his castle". This great passion for privacy, the desire of families to live as independent, self-contained units has had a big impact on housing.

In England there has been, for hundreds of years, a general reaction against communal living. The dominant housing unit has been the individualized family house, perhaps built in a terrace, but intended, when built, to be a one-family house. The social developments which took place in terraces are a part of English folklore. They became centres of solidarity and mutual aid. The television programme *Coronation Street*, produced by Granada TV, is concerned with the everyday life of people in a terraced street in the north-west of England. It is the best contemporary example of the belief that the inhabitants of such environments have greater closeness and friendship than people who live in different housing arrangements. Everybody seems to be free to enter everyone else's house, whether it be for a chat or a cup of sugar. As terraced areas like Coronation Street are redeveloped, and the people moved to tower-block flats, the community spirit seems to wither. Although the tower block is only a vertical terrace, it lacks the street and the front step as a meeting-place. There does seem, in England, to be a strong desire for low-level housing, and if possible in separate units. The dream of the average city-dweller is for his own semi-detached, with a pocket of garden, like a fragment of a great estate. Yet, cross the border to Scotland, and high-density communal life has long been common and accepted as normal. In the same way, European countries think of apartment life as the norm. The explanation for these differences is difficult to pin down, but its effect is great. The decline in tower-block construction in England is largely explained by adverse social attitudes.

Birth rates, death rates and the growth of the towns

Many of the changes which this book touches on are the result of variations in the numbers, composition and character of our population. These in themselves reflect social changes. The size and organization of the family is now largely a matter of personal choice – with better family planning techniques, and their widespread availability, most people are able to decide on the number of children they have. In the last century, this freedom was not widely available, and family size and the population depended on a delicate balance between life and death. From the beginning of the century, better medicine has meant that death rates have fallen sharply. A simple measure used to compare statistics of death is the Crude Death Rate (CDR), which is calculated for any one year as

$$\frac{\text{Number of deaths in any one year}}{\text{Total population at midpoint of the year}} \times 1000$$

The CDR in urban areas at the beginning of the nineteenth century was often thirty-five to forty per thousand, as high as in any of the Third World countries today. Table VII shows the decline over the period of the last hundred years. The birth rate, however, stayed high and this caused a tremendous boom in population. The effect upon the towns was to further increase densities, and the population explosion was responsible for generating the worst of the social conditions of the last century. To cope with the problems thrown up, the Public Health and other Acts were passed, but these, in many cases, made the problems bigger because they further decreased the CDR. We may criticize nineteenth-century bye-law housing for cramming people into limited spaces, but cheap high-density housing was the only way of coping with the pressure of numbers.

Table VII Crude birth and death rates for England and Wales 1861–1971		
Rates are given in births, or deaths, per thousand of the population		
Year	Crude birth rate	Crude death rate
1861	34·6	21·6
1871	35·0	22·6
1881	33·9	18·9
1891	31·4	20·2
1901	28·5	16·9
1911	24·4	14·6
1921	22·4	12·1
1931	15·8	12·3
1941	15·0	13·5
1951	15·6	11·9
1961	17·6	11·8
1964	18·5	11·3
1965	18·1	11·5
1966	17·7	11·8
1971	15·9	11·4

Fig. 56   **Houses and family size. Even ordinary houses reflected growth in family size. These have dormer attics for the children. Note also the decoration, mixtures of different coloured bricks (polychrome) arranged in bands and as contrasts in the** *voussoir* **(wedge-shaped) bricks forming the arches over the windows. The roof is of the mansard type, underneath the gutters are bricks arranged to produce dentilations, derived from Classical forms. The dormers are also decorated with fancy barge-boards hiding the edge of the rafters. One other point of interest is the number of chimneys, which gives an indication of the number of rooms. In this case, each house has at least six rooms, twelve pots being shared on one stack.**

		Table VIII Total British population and rates of increase			
Year	Est. total pop. (millions)	Av. annual rate of increase %	Year	Est. total pop. (millions)	Av. annual rate of increase %
1801	10·5	1·4	1901	37·0	0·7
1821	14·1	1·4	1921	42·8	0·4
1841	18·5	1·2	1941	47·2	0·5
1861	23·1	1·2	1961	52·3	0·5
1881	29·7	1·1	1971	55·7	—

			Table IX Percentage of population in various age-groups, Britain, 1841–1971				
Year	0–14	15–29	30–44	45–59	60–74	75 +	Total
1841	36·2	27·8	18·4	10·4	5·8	1·4	100·0
1861	35·7	26·5	18·6	11·7	6·1	1·4	100·0
1881	36·5	26·7	17·9	11·4	6·1	1·4	100·0
1901	32·5	28·3	19·7	12·1	6·0	1·4	100·0
1921	28·0	25·5	21·2	15·9	7·7	1·7	100·0
1941	21·4	24·4	23·2	17·5	11·1	2·4	100·0
1961	22·9	19·4	20·1	20·3	13·0	4·3	100·0
1971	24·2	20·8	17·6	20·7	11·9	4·8	100·0

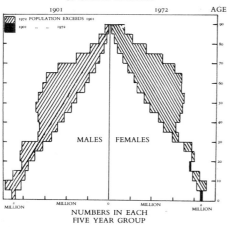

SEX AND AGE STRUCTURE
OF UNITED KINGDOM

NUMBERS IN EACH
FIVE YEAR GROUP

Table VIII:

With an annual percent increase of 0·5, the population doubles every 139 years.

With an annual percent increase of 0·8, the population doubles every 87 years.

With an annual percent increase of 1·0, the population doubles every 70 years.

With an annual percent increase of 2·0, the population doubles every 35 years.

Left: Fig. 57   **The sex and age structure of the UK, 1901 and 1972.**

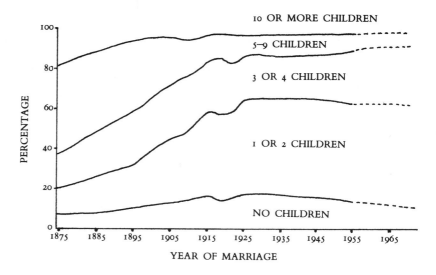

Right: Fig. 58   **Percentage of families of various sizes Britain 1875–1955.** The beginning of the graph shows that less than forty per cent of families had four children or less (see where the lines begin on the vertical axis). Now over eighty per cent of families are in that grouping. Because recent families may not be complete, the percentages are shown in broken lines and should be treated only as trends.

After the 1870s, birth rates began to fall, partly because family planning information became more freely available to all people. Before 1875 publishers were often prosecuted for selling books which gave very sensible advice on birth control, which we would consider very tame today but which was viewed as legally obscene at that time. However, in that year, two reformers, Charles Bradlaugh (1833–91) and Annie Besant (1847–1933), were sent to trial for selling such material: at the Old Bailey they fought their own case, won, and literature on birth control practice became more widely available. This new knowledge had a big impact on many middle-class families who were becoming more and more concerned with the size of their families. Groups of eight or ten children often meant that large portions of the family income went towards education or to providing marriage settlements. (The working-class response came later.) Smaller families had a marked effect on the urban landscape, especially in housing. The late Victorian and Edwardian family house with six or eight bedrooms gradually gave way, from the 1920s onward, to the three- or four-bedroomed house. This trend was reinforced as fewer and fewer families could afford to employ servants. For the poor, smaller families came later, and in their case it meant not smaller houses for houses were a minimum size already, but an end to children sleeping three and four to a bed.

Crude Birth Rates (calculated in a similar way as the CDR) for the British population fell in a series of stages, and the results are set out in Figure 58 which shows the changes in family size over part of the hundred years to 1955. Families may have grown smaller, but the population continued rising. The number of families, each wanting its own house, increased dramatically. If each of them was to have a house, then our urban areas had to expand in some way, either upwards or outwards, and quickly. For example, in 1951, Great Britain had a population of 48·9

million, with 14·6 million private households. In 1971, with a population 53·8 million, an increase of approximately ten per cent, there were 18·2 million households, almost twenty-five per cent more.

Increasing age

As families become smaller, the age structure of the population changes. Table IX shows the percentage of the population in various age groups since 1841; Figure 57 uses population pyramids to compare two periods of time. There is today a far higher proportion of people in the older age groups than there used to be. In the nineteenth century, old people were normally cared for as part of the "extended family", perhaps three or four generations living together in one house. This is no longer the rule. More and more houses are built nowadays specially for the aged, often with their own community developments. Again, this fragmentation of families leads to expansion and pressure for space on the urban surface. The other fact which emerges from the statistics is the smaller numbers of the young. This has an effect in that it is directly reflected in the need for schools, playgrounds and play areas.

Population and planning

Planners have to build for future families and communities, and sometimes their plans may take twenty years to complete. Changes in birth and death rates, in the composition and total of the population, are crucial to their calculations of how many homes and social facilities future developments are to have. Unfortunately for them, they cannot predict with accuracy people's attitudes. The recent rapid fall in the birth rate from the peak of the 1960s has meant that many estimates and plans for the future have had to be revised. If the present trend in birth rates continues, we may even have too many schools, twenty years from now.

9 Planning

Below: Fig. 59   Be it ever so well planned, it's not necessarily like home. Hulme, Manchester.

So far, in this book, the forces which shape our surroundings have been pictured as being largely under the control of individuals. Men with enough money have been able to design and build to their own desires. Lesser mortals have to buy or rent what is already available, according to their means. A family environment is, in this analysis, largely related to its income. But this type of economic free-for-all is not the system in force today. Increasingly, our environment, both urban and rural, is "planned" by central or by local government. Most of the urban landscape is controlled. Regulations govern the material, size and internal organization of our buildings and we have already discussed some of the legislation which affects our roads.

The growth of planning control has been gradual and marked by great controversy. "The liberty of the individual" is at stake, cry the opponents of central planning. For this reason, its growth has been opposed, sometimes by supporters of liberty in general, but also by those who have suddenly found their own particular freedoms threatened. The nineteenth-century Public Health Acts, for example, were viewed as an invasion of liberty by the slum landlords.

It is not quite true to suggest that planning always works for the benefit of the poor against the rich, or that it always results in an improvement of the environment. Every period of history has its legislation based on social control, and the direction of control reflects the beliefs of those who frame the regulations. The improvements in urban conditions in the nineteenth century were often made in the face of the violent and public disapproval of famous people. Today, few would accept that a fall in profits could be a valid reason for opposing the improvement of low-quality housing or difficult and dangerous working conditions, yet this was a frequent objection made in the last century. Now we hear more of the loss of personal liberty in terms of amenity, as when motorways are routed through areas of outstanding beauty.

The Romans were the first "town planners" to operate in Britain, building the core areas of towns and cities such as York, Bath, London and Leicester. They sometimes used standardized plans whose uniform organization still remains in the present lay-out. However, in many cases their efforts were abandoned and it was not until early medieval times that towns were "planned" once again. The Normans, and later Edward I, planned and built a number of fortified towns along the borders of Wales, England and Scotland. Once again, the remnants of these can be seen in their modern successors. But one of the major influences controlling most of our towns came in the eleventh century, when the first legislative steps were taken to deal with the worst of medieval urban problems: fire. Fire prevention was critical in the medieval town. For hundreds of years it was the most important single influence in the control of the urban landscape. We can use it as an example of how past attitudes and responses continue to mould our environment, for fire regulations still exercise a major restraining influence on the raw material and design of our surroundings.

Guide to further study

There is little information easily available on the effect and importance of fire. Parts of the architectural books in chapters five and six give the effects of fire legislation upon style and materials. An official publication on the subject is

> S. B. Hamilton, *A Short History of the Structural Fire Protection of Building* (HMSO).

The influence of fire legislation on the town and its buildings can be studied in terms of contrasting materials and in modern construction the various height limitations. It may be possible to see some of the original fire insurance plaques, made of lead, copper or iron, set on the wall with the policy number engraved on them.

Study 7 Fire and its impact

Fire and the medieval town

Eight hundred years ago, British town buildings were mainly timber-framed. Wood was easily obtained locally and joinery was less expensive than masonry. Wooden buildings were cheaper and quicker to construct than stone ones. Their biggest defect was that they were more prone to damage by fire. This was made more of a danger by the building methods used. Tall buildings with timber frames were unstable. They tended to spread and eventually collapse. The upper storeys of the buildings usually used jetty construction (see Figure 60). In this the upper frames were set out, beyond the line of the lower, and the weight on the interior floors would be balanced by the overhang. On this principle, three- and four-storey buildings could be erected with a fair degree of stability. But, as they rose, they stuck out further and further from the ground-floor building line. The top storeys of opposite houses would almost meet across the narrow streets. Fires would spread rapidly, travelling across straw-thatched roofs and eating through the timber frames.

In the fight against the dangers of fire, London led the way for the rest of Britain. It pioneered most of the legislation on fire control and legislation, prompted by the scale of its own disasters. London had been destroyed by fire repeatedly, dating from Boudicca's deliberate burning of AD 61. In the eleventh and twelfth centuries, the fires of 1077, 1087 and 1161 caused great damage. In 1189, Henry Fitz Alwyn, first Mayor of London, set out the London Assize, a series of bye-laws relating mainly to fire prevention. Their main demand was that the party walls between houses should be at least 3 feet thick and 16 feet high, to stop the spread of fire. In 1212, after another fire, thatched roofs were forbidden, their place taken by tiles, lead, wooden shingles or boards. Also, ale-houses were prohibited in the City of London, unless they were built of stone, an early example of controlling dangerous trades.

The Great Fire and the rebuilding of London

Very little further control occurred before 1667, the year after the Great Fire. Up until this time, most buildings were still timber-framed, with lath-and-plaster infilling. The city was now so big, that a fire would no longer endanger just a few hundred houses but tens of thousands. The Great Fire of 1666 destroyed thirteen thousand houses, eighty per cent of the city. The response to this damage was rapid and, by the next year, the Act for the Rebuilding of the City of London had been passed. Strict controls were put upon the replacement buildings so that fire dangers would not be inbuilt into the new city. In the first plans, only four types of house were allowed, each of controlled dimensions, but

Below: Fig. 60   Jetty construction. By using this method, the weight upon the floor at (B) was balanced by the weight of the projecting wall at (A). A heavy, carved beam – the *bressummer* (C) was a main support and the overhang of the jetty was supported by carved brackets called *modillions* (D).

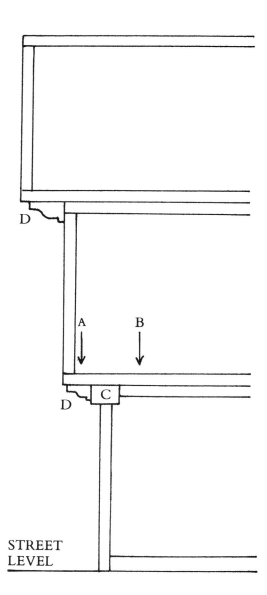

STREET
LEVEL

these standards were later abandoned. There were stringent regulations on wall thickness, timber sizes and many other details. If the building failed to comply with the regulations, it could be torn down. Anyone infringing them could be imprisoned. Apart from the rebuilding of properties, there were schemes for widening streets and replacing certain important public structures destroyed in the fire. St Paul's Cathedral is most notable of those still standing. Part of the rebuilding of the city was financed by a tax on "sea-coal" delivered to London, which continued for twenty years.

There were still localized fires to be dealt with and the regulations were constantly being up-dated. In 1707, an Act prohibited overhanging eaves on future buildings and stipulated that the walls of houses were to be extended not less than eighteen inches (forty-five centimetres) above the roof. This explains why, in films, burglars crossing London's Georgian skyline are always having to jump over walls when escaping across the roof-tops. It also helps to explain the characteristic frontage of Queen Anne and Regency houses with low-angle roofs, hidden behind a stone cornice. The uniformity of building style we see in the late eighteenth century is largely due to fire regulations. The relationship between street width and building height, the parapets and cornices, the recessed window frame and the proportion of window to wall were all the result of legislation. Throughout the century, more preventive Acts appeared, dealing particularly with the type and thickness of walls; regulations also began to appear to help firefighting and control. London parishes had been maintaining fire pumps throughout the eighteenth century, but the London Building Act of 1774 made them compulsory, as well as virtually banning the use of timber on the exposed surfaces of buildings. From this time on, the technical nature of firefighting became an important factor in the design of new areas. Water supply and the need to rescue people from burning buildings were matters that all architects were now forced to consider in their calculations.

Firefighting and its impact on the skyline

The firemen of the time were usually volunteers and it was not until the 1830s that regular fire-brigades were organized, chiefly by insurance companies wishing to reduce their losses. For example, the London Fire Brigade, formed in 1832, was responsible to the companies until 1866, when it was taken over by the Metropolitan Board. Its task was not made any easier by the lack of water in the capital; many areas still relied on wooden water mains and it was not until the 1875 Public Health Act that local authorities were compelled to provide the fire hydrant access which we still use today. Technically the fire-brigades were poorly-equipped, the combination of short escape-ladders and a low water pressure meant that they were rarely capable of fighting a fire more than 25 metres from the ground. Because of the dangers implied in this, London in the 1850s

Above: Fig. 61   Victorian fire-regulated offices. Very ornamental, but they were prevented from making the best use of their area by the fire regulations of the time. The upper storey marks the limit of fire-fighting efficiency until the 1930s.

Above: Fig. 63   Fire regulations and styles. These early nineteenth-century buildings have many features controlled by legislation designed to hinder the spread of fire. The windows are set back in the frame, the cornice is of stone, the height is limited and behind the parapet of the right-hand one, the attics in the mansard roof have a means of escape in case of fire.

Left: Fig. 62   Even at the end of the nineteenth century fire was still a hazard, so that large vaults like this one were built to store goods and furniture in safety.

had an absolute height restriction of eighty feet (27·4 metres) on its new buildings. The London Building Act of 1894 limited the height of the external walls of buildings to this figure and this had the effect of rigidly controlling the vertical expansion of buildings. The only exception was in offices, where a further two storeys could be built in the roof, as long as there was a means of escape from fire. These dormer-windowed floors can still be seen in the Victorian office blocks that are left. The effect of the limitations of firefighting techniques continued to be a major factor in height control for many years. Until 1939, the height of firefighting ladders was the most important single influence affecting controls on vertical expansion.

At the same time, experiments in new fire-resistant materials led to changes in styles and constituents. Asbestos-cement and "corrugated iron" (zinc and asbestos) came to be used in thousands of cheaper buildings this century, such as the post-1945 "pre-fab" housing. Partly as a result of air raids during the Second World War, firefighting techniques improved and new hydraulic machinery allowed rescue at greater heights. Even so, there are technical limitations to the heights at which firefighting and rescue can go on; high-rise offices and apartment blocks are often beyond the range of modern equipment, whose limit is normally 110 feet (34 metres). If they seem to have outgrown the restrictions, in fact controls still operate, although in a different way. Government Building Regulations severely control all properties, and if people cannot easily be rescued from great heights, then the buildings must be as fire-proof as possible. The main hazard is the spread of fire and here the most useful device is to place the buildings as far apart as possible. Part of the organization of tower-block communities can be explained by this. If this is impossible, as it may be in city centres, then architects have to use fire-proof materials; for example, it is illegal in Britain to build a house entirely from timber. The design of buildings, especially large ones, is arranged so that they form a series of compartments, each of which can be isolated to prevent the spread of fire. The regulation of building material and design covers every aspect of the urban scene. Multi-storey car parks are classed as petroleum stores, with an assessed potential of 4 gallons (18 litres) of petrol per vehicle space. Their bare, gaunt outlines are due to the necessity of building them in fire-resisting, reinforced concrete and their low elevation is due to the need for easy access and escape.

10 The ideal community

If fire was the major control affecting the urban environment for several hundred years, it was progressively replaced by legislation dealing with health. It might also be argued that in the late sixteenth and seventeenth centuries there was a standardization brought about by literature. The designs of influential architects began to circulate as duplicated pattern-books, which any moderately-skilled builder could copy. The better reproductions were of neo-Classical "Great Houses", but they also affected the ordinary town house, bringing a degree of uniformity to Georgian terraces throughout the country. In the nineteenth century, influential works such as the *Encyclopaedia of Cottage, Farm and Villa Architecture* (1832) by John Claudius Loudon (1783–1843) gave styles and patterns for everything from house fronts to garden seats. This type of standardization was a voluntary one, but the biggest influences have been those which have been obligatory, demanded by legislation.

It has been pointed out previously that Public Health and Housing Acts controlled certain aspects of low-income housing in the nineteenth century. At the same time, these Acts referred equally to all sections of the urban area and to all classes. The provisions of the main pieces of legislation which dealt with urban design are shown on page 21. It can be seen how comprehensive they were. Together they accelerated the process of evolution which has produced our present towns and cities. They dealt with housing density, design, water supply, size of rooms, width of streets, sewerage and many other critical factors. The improvements contained within the Acts were often the creations of individuals who pressed for change in the face of powerful opposition. The most influential of these, Edwin Chadwick (1801–90), presented to the British public most of the unsavoury statistics and details which forced through the passage of the various measures. He thought that the poor in towns should have some of the care which they had previously enjoyed in more rural societies. His major document, *An Enquiry into the Sanitary Condition of the Labouring Population of Great Britain*, published in 1842, argued that "the wealthy and educated gradually withdrew themselves from these close and crowded communities; which thus stand more and more in need of some superintending paternal care". Chadwick saw it as his duty to apply maximum pressure for control and it was largely through his evidence that the first major Public Health Act was carried through in 1848.

While Chadwick, and later Lord Shaftesbury (1801–85), argued for better national controls, other people had for a long time been convinced that improvements could best be organized on a local scale, within small communities. Some schemes were based on a desire to maintain close physical links between workers and masters, so that in living close to one another they might produce better social relationships. This was an early type of socialist approach to urban design. However, most of the plans were built on the premise that if the workers were well-housed and living in pleasant surroundings they were likely to be more content at work, with fewer labour troubles. Although some of the movements and developments were relatively short-lived, they helped make planning more acceptable. The first expression of the movement began in 1792, when David Dale (1739–1806) built the community of New Lanark in Scotland. Centred on textile employment, it provided, for its time, high-quality two- or three-storeyed, stone tenements, let for a rent which the workers could afford, without affecting their ability to buy food. Its significance as an experiment in planning began in 1799, when Robert Owen (1771–1858), an admirer of the principles of the French Revolution, took charge and placed a greater emphasis on social improvement. He proposed schemes for model industrial villages, based on a strong sense of community and he is also credited with being the first influential figure to attempt to spread birth control techniques amongst working people. Having seen, on his travels in southern France, the relationship between small family size and prosperity, he thought it essential that his workers should have the same freedom of choice as French peasants.

Most of the later community plans were less socialistic in attitude, more concerned with providing a relatively docile working force. The "garden village" of Price's Candle Works at Bromborough was one of the first employer-built settlements with ideas on the advantages of open spaces and gardens for its workers. At the same time Saltaire, a model village, was being built in the West Riding by Titus Salt (1803–76). This was a textile community, centred on the mill, and the buildings are still in use today. It is now somewhat more liberal than its Victorian predecessor, allowing public houses within its area. Some of the plans, such as that for the model town of Victoria conceived by James Silk Buckingham (1786–1855), were never translated into bricks and mortar and remained drawing-board Utopias. The Garden Suburbs of Lever at Port Sunlight and Cadbury at Bournville came later, setting new standards,

much of the housing being of better quality and design than most middle-class dwellings elsewhere. Even culture was given to the workers, with museums and art galleries!

Although the developments were only local, their success and acceptance led to a changing attitude towards the way communities developed. In the twentieth century, this included, not only an element of control, but also, a positive attitude where communities were seen as not only needing certain standards of sanitation but also ideas as to how people should live in the widest sense. We shall see how the ideas of the first social planners grew, until now we use terms such as social engineering, deciding how planning measures affect the quality of people's lives. This is not planning, or control, as it would have been visualized in the nineteenth century, and it marks a significant difference between the attitudes of the two periods.

Guide to further study: see page 81

Left: Fig. 64   **A block of flats in Robert Owen's community of New Lanark.**

Below: Fig. 65   **Modern tenement life.**

Study 8 Planning the landscape

The growth of national planning

By the end of the nineteenth century, local councils had acquired, often unwillingly, great powers of control. In many cases they were not forced to use them and, as in the early Public Health Acts and the power to build council dwellings, they often ignored their responsibilities. It is very easy to portray the local councils as a conspiracy of land-lords and property owners, fighting their own rearguard action against social progress. This view overstates the case, although powerful factions did delay changes as long as possible.

The twentieth century has seen a decline in local authorities' power to initiate and determine legislation and national government has become considerably more powerful. In the last century, there were some progressive and some backward councils, but today most major planning decisions are taken at a national level. Local councils have much less power to frustrate the intentions of the central authority. The effect of social planning is, therefore, much more uniformly felt across the country.

We have already seen how the role of government intervention in housing has developed, in study one, page 16. There we dealt in particular with low-income housing and the increasing government control was clear. The same growth in power and influence is apparent in other sectors, for planning cannot only deal with the quality of life of one particular social group, or one section of the community. It has to deal with all matters affecting people's life and work in the whole of the urban area. One of the main ways in which planning has affected urban areas has been in terms of their size and growth. At the start of the nineteenth century towns and cities were compact. As transport improvements allowed them to expand, problems began to result from their uncontrolled growth. If the process of urban expansion had continued, without the checks which the planners have produced, we would have a very different urban and rural landscape today.

Urban sprawl

We saw in chapter four the impact of transport as a factor in the rate of urban expansion. Over the last hundred years, the growth of planning machinery has been almost equally important, sometimes contributing to growth and sometimes to restriction. From medieval times, town buildings had been huddled together, each one pressed closely to the next. While this was excellent for protection against cold, it made the spread of fire and disease much easier. Viewing the crowded slums of Victorian England, with over 200 houses to the hectare (80 to the acre), supporters of reform saw that a decrease in housing density would be one way of fighting disease. After the 1875 Public Health Act, the density of the new, bye-law terraces was planned to be not more than 125 to the hectare (50 to the acre). If there were to be fewer houses built to the hectare, then the solution to housing the increasing population of the time had to lie in expanding the area of the towns and cities.

As we have seen, the middle classes were already on the move, followed by the skilled tradesmen. Even though the 1890s brought a check to the growth of British prosperity, urban expansion continued up till the First World War. After it, new developments brought a faster rate of growth. The Tudor Walters Report of 1918 recommended that new working-class housing should be built at densities not exceeding 12 houses per acre (30 per hectare). Addison's Act of 1919 required local authorities to submit plans for housing to fill the gaps which were apparent in most of our towns and cities. These plans were submitted to the Ministry of Health and were not accepted if they exceeded the Tudor Walters density. Speculative builders were already producing semi-detached properties at densities much less than this.

Almost all the new local authority housing was built outside the existing area and here they competed with the private market. This competition was fiercest for sites with easy access to main roads, a factor of great attraction to the growing army of road commuters, whose numbers grew particularly in the 1930s, when the private motor car became cheap enough for the mass of professional people. The railways lost their dominance and instead thousands of "desirable" suburban semi's strung out along the main roads became the aim of the white-collar workers. These houses spread rapidly, using the existing main-road pattern and they grew like tentacles from the body of the town. Few houses were built into the country away from the main road and the term "ribbon development" was used to describe the results.

While access to the main road at the front, and views of open fields at the back, were obvious attractions to the new settlers, the advantages to society in general were less obvious. The growth of this pattern extended lines of public services, buses, water supply and sewerage; the extension was expensive, serving comparatively few people. It also brought some of the intrusions of urban life, such as noise and "wirescape", into the decreasing areas of rural land. Together with ribbon development, the main body of the towns also grew, as larger and larger housing estates were built, using relatively cheap rural land and eating into our agricultural area. It became possible to predict the coalescence of major urban areas, joining first along the ribbons, and later fusing into one continuous built-up zone.

Above: Fig. 66   **Ribbon development near Bromsgrove, Worcestershire.**

By the 1950s this type of feature had arrived in the USA, where a continuous urbanized area emerged, stretching over three hundred kilometres from New York to Baltimore, and given the name Megalopolis by the geographer Jean Gottman (b. 1915).

Saving the countryside from suburbia

Legislation to limit this type of growth came soon after the period of maximum expansion. In fact, from 1909, local authorities had the power to acquire land up to 666 feet (203 metres) from either side of new roads, but few of them did so. In 1935, the Restriction of Ribbon Development Act laid down that all new plans within 225 feet (68 metres) of the middle of classified roads, had to have local authority approval. But the local authorities themselves were closely involved in expansion, building their council houses on the edges of the towns. Although ribbon development slowed, estate building, responsible for the greatest growth in area, continued as before. At the outbreak of the Second World War, one third of the houses in Britain had been built since 1919, most of them in areas which had previously been farmland, or some other form of open space. There were no effective powers to stop the expansion.

By 1945, the Government had accepted that the growth of our largest cities should be restricted. The 1947 Town and Country Planning Act introduced widespread changes which meant that all development needed planning permission. Where expansion had to take place, it was to be channelled into specific areas and not allowed to sprawl over the countryside. The excess population from the towns, or overspill, was to be rehoused in new and expanded towns. The New Towns Act of 1947 introduced the first generation of them. Expanded towns, small towns making overspill arrangements with larger ones, came after the Town Development Act of 1952. London had the most pressing problems because of its vast size and its rapid rate of growth. Its New Towns – Basildon, Bracknell, Crawley, Harlow, Hatfield, Hemel Hempstead, Stevenage and Welwyn – were mostly built away from the metropolis, and a Green Belt was created, eleven to sixteen kilometres wide (seven to ten miles). In this area, residential and industrial growth was to be particularly restricted and it was hoped, in this way, to halt the advance of the capital. Recent developments in the south-east have seen the zone outside the Green Belt, the outer metropolitan area, grow rapidly, both because of the New Towns and thriving industrial and residential centres. Other conurbations, such as those centred on Glasgow and Liverpool, have similar developments, with New Towns and industrial-estate housing being the fastest-growing sections of the regions. Sometimes it results in the siphoning-off of the youngest and most energetic of the urban population, leaving behind the old and less ambitious.

As well as general controls on expansion, more and more of our urban landscape has become subject to legislation.

Later in the book, we shall see more of the details. People are often unaware of the powers which control them, until they wish to build a garage on their house, or put a dormer window in their roof or an illuminated sign outside their shop. There are planning controls on most building activity, sometimes on seemingly trivial details. Some people react to this as an intrusion on personal liberty, or fear the increasing standardization in our lives. The effects of social planning have not all been beneficial. It has allowed the destruction of many buildings which should have been saved, and has encouraged many projects it might have been wiser to control. But even its most severe critics would find it difficult to argue that we would have made the same advances in the quality of our environment if the only controls on progress had remained economic ones.

Below: Fig. 67 **The planning of London's growth. In 1944 the Greater London Plan was published. It was one of the first attempts to deal with the dangers involved in uncontrolled urban growth. Prepared by Sir Patrick Abercrombie (1879–1957), it showed how the problems could be dealt with by de-centralization, moving industries and people away from the city into new communities. The "new satellite towns" on the Plan became the New Towns of the London region.**

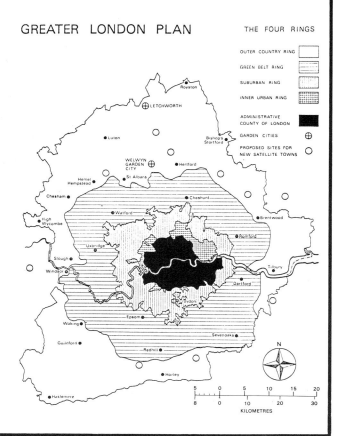

GREATER LONDON PLAN

THE FOUR RINGS

OUTER COUNTRY RING

GREEN BELT RING

SUBURBAN RING

INNER URBAN RING

ADMINISTRATIVE COUNTY OF LONDON

GARDEN CITIES

PROPOSED SITES FOR NEW SATELLITE TOWNS

11 The town centre

Each of the themes examined so far has been viewed in isolation; any connection between them has been accidental. But they do interact, for every change made to the urban environment causes a chain of reactions. The remaining sections of this book deal not with separate themes but with geographical areas. Firstly, the different parts of the urban area will be looked at, to see how the various factors at work together produce the visible environment. And in the final section we will see how one real town has developed, and how its features have formed and changed.

Most of the material presented so far has concentrated on housing as a feature in the urban area. There is some logic to this, in that houses make up a large majority of the buildings in any town or city. However, the reasons for the existence and growth of each period of urban change often lie in the central core. We have seen how economic forces tend to concentrate profit-making functions in Central Areas. In the Industrial Revolution factories were also common in the centres, rising, like the offices and shops, from the remains of the medieval buildings. In the last hundred years, there have been fewer and fewer factories in urban centres, for a number of reasons. Firms have needed larger premises as they have increasingly brought many processes together under one roof. The processes themselves, often carried out on the assembly-line principle, have needed large, single-storeyed buildings, designed for horizontal movement. The price of land in Central Areas makes such developments expensive, and unusual. Also, the transport situation has changed, and nearness to railway termini and sidings has become less of an attractive influence. New industrial developments often prefer to be in perimeter locations, in trading estates on outer ring roads, or near to motorway junctions. There has also been the greater mobility of workers, which has allowed the industries to move out, knowing that their work force would be able to follow them. The days of the nineteenth-century mill situation, when workers lived within the shadow of the chimney, have largely disappeared. The industries which do remain in town centres are of a well-defined character. They are either the small craft industries such as bespoke tailoring, or the essentially centralized ones, newspaper printing being the best example.

Today's Central Areas have certain identifying characteristics but their scale varies considerably with the overall size of the urban area. It may be an exaggeration to even use the term Central Area in a small market town, where there may only be one main street as a focus of retail

and service trades. In this case, the specializations implied in the term Central Area disappear within the space of a few minutes' walk. Not so in the large city. Here the scale, the economic specialization, the concentration of traffic and pedestrians all combine to give a character, a collection of features which mark out the area from all others. Attempts to define what the centre is, and where it ends, are common in urban literature. The Americans, who have produced most of the studies, use the term Central Business District or, more recently, Downtown. They define the zone as one which is organized for profit, dominated by functions which need to be in the centre in order to maximize their income. In Britain, this definition is not an entirely satisfactory one. Many of our central buildings, such as town halls, are concerned with administration or, as in the case of libraries and museums, they offer a public service. There is also the fact that many of our older towns contain groups of buildings which remain because we wish to conserve them, even though they are not the most profitable

Right: Fig. 68 **Work and home. It has been the improved mobility of the twentieth century which has made the home-next-to-factory arrangement more unusual.**

use of the land. However, it is true to say that, in most cases, the larger Central Areas are characterized by uses which concentrate on the profit motive.

The features which set the centre apart from the rest of the urban area are the size and shape of the buildings, the specialization of their uses and the concentration of transport factors. The explanation for their presence comes from a mixture of economic and historical reasons. Often the present centre is built upon the area of the medieval core. As the urban area grew, housing and industry were forced outward and demand for land in the centre encouraged vertical growth of the buildings. In the nineteenth century, railway stations were normally built on the perimeter of the existing centre, reinforcing its attraction. In the twentieth, the mobility of the population allowed it to retain its power. As roads and railway lines ended or met near the centre, the centres continued to draw in certain specialized users. A full list of the range of

functions attracted to the core would be too lengthy to include, but there are a number which are common to all town centres.

Even small towns show a clustering of solicitors, estate agents, insurance offices, shoe and dress shops. Add to these larger-scale functions, such as town halls, company head-offices and department stores, and the characteristics of Central Areas of large urban units begin to emerge. The more important the centre, the greater demand there is for space. In small towns, the centre is relatively compact, but of low elevation. In larger towns, building heights in the Centre Area increase.

The advantage that high-rise buildings give to a centre is to concentrate activities and thus save travelling time and expense. It is very unlikely that town centres and city Central Areas would have grown to be such specialized zones, if it had not been for the high-rise building, which has made them such intensive, compact units.

Below: Fig. 69   **Central Area characteristics. Size is the most obvious feature, with development making maximum use of the precious land.**

Study 9 The development of tall buildings

Their slow rate of growth

There is little evidence of buildings taller than four or five storeys in medieval times. Most of them had upper floors of timber-framed, jetty construction, which were of limited stability. In any case, there was less demand for central space and less pressure on the land. By the sixteenth and seventeenth centuries, London and Edinburgh had ten and twelve storey buildings, but these were exceptional. It was the nineteenth century, with its improved technology and increasing demand for land, which produced the medium-rise, older sections of our Central Areas. The new-style glass and concrete box-buildings have grown up mainly in the last thirty years.

At the beginning of the last century newer and larger buildings were appearing in most of the town centres. The neo-Classical style was little used for tall structures, their height would destroy what were thought to be "correct" proportions. Most town-centre commercial buildings come in a Gothic form, although the largest and tallest ones are often plain and undecorated, having relatively humble functions such as warehouses, or mills. They were normally of brick or stone, but the materials themselves imposed restrictions on the height of the features. The scaffolding used was wooden and expensive to assemble to any great height. Mechanical handling of materials was poorly developed, although the delightfully-named "Dr Spurgin's Machine for Hoisting Bricks, Mortar, etc." was used during the building of the Houses of Parliament (1840–65). The materials were only as strong as the mortar which held them together. In many cases, there did not seem any point in building high; it only made you more isolated, unless you wished to spend all your time rushing up and down stairs. Business was still conducted on a personal basis, over coffee, or a glass of port.

By 1800, cast iron was being used in some buildings as a supporting framework, but it was generally held to be unreliable. For the most part the brick or stone acted as the supporting, or load-bearing, section. Its strength was responsible for holding the building up, and for supporting the weight on the floors. It was not until better methods of production made good iron and steel cheaper, that an iron or steel framework became widely used as the sole support. An important date here was the introduction of the Bessemer process in 1868. This enabled the rapid and cheap conversion of pig-iron into mild steel, which was the main material for reinforcing buildings. Other materials important for increasing building height developed during the period. The French were responsible for most of the work involved in the development of concrete, especially from 1850 onwards. Joseph Monier (1823–1906) patented

reinforced concrete in 1867, François Hennebique (1842–1921) was building concrete bridges by the 1880s, and Eugène Freyssinet (1879–1962) developed pre-stressed concrete, after seeing reinforced concrete structures show great cracks due to stress. Concrete became the chief material of architects in the twentieth century, and was essential to the cheap and rapid construction of high-rise blocks. A German, Walter Gropius (1883–1969), was largely responsible for using concrete in modern styling. The buildings which resulted were almost all the "curtain wall" variety, where the framework is hidden behind an external screen, usually of glass and aluminium. The first British building to use curtain walling was the Peter Jones store in London; this was in 1936, many years after its introduction in Western Europe. This was a common trend in high-rise development; the British have been very slow in adopting new ideas, if they originated from abroad.

Chicago and the "high-rise"

The dominant feature of Central Area buildings is not so much the material as the height. Once again, the major innovations came from other countries, in this case from North America, and in particular from Chicago. In the middle of the nineteenth century, "Chicago construction" meant a light frame, made up of stocks and boards which were nailed together. In the Mid-West, this method was widely used in house construction. But Chicago was soon to become famous for a very different type of building. By the 1860s Chicago was mushrooming as a business centre and new offices were rising throughout the Loop, the core of the city, so-called because it lies in a bend of the Chicago river. Among the architects practising there, was William le Baron Jenney (1832–1907), known as "Major" Jenney. In 1883 construction began on his Home Insurance Building. It was of a revolutionary design, using a cast-iron frame for the first six floors, and steel for the remaining four. This metal "skeleton" was fully load-bearing, and so the exterior could be a light façade of brick. Because it carried no weight, this façade was built in thin piers, enclosing and supporting large window spaces. The structure was strong, fireproof, and allowed in plenty of light. It was the fore-runner of most of our modern offices. By the 1890s Louis Sullivan (1856–1924) was designing offices of up to seventeen storeys high, using Jenney's principles. The high-rise building itself developed in Chicago and spread from the USA to Europe, but its widespread use depended on the introduction of other new techniques, without which the tall building would have been commercially unworkable.

There was no point in having seventeen-storey offices if the customer had to climb seventeen flights of stairs to the

Above left: Fig. 70   Early high-rise. Nineteenth-century British buildings would use a cast-iron frame, together with a load-bearing outer wall. This one, in the process of demolition, shows the organization well.

Above right: Fig. 71   British styles. These are early twentieth-century high-rise. The right-hand one is still strongly influenced by Classical design, the left-hand one is important as the first large British building of reinforced concrete, described when it was built as the best example of concrete construction in the world.

top and businessmen had to dash between floors to see their associates. The goods lift was in fairly common use in the USA by 1850, using hydraulic motors and cages on the end of steel ropes. They were generally considered to be unsafe until, in 1853, Elisha Otis (1811–61) installed a safety device in his lifts. He used a system of ratchets and levers which engaged and stopped the lift if by any chance the rope broke. The Otis family later went into partnership with Jenney, and the Leiter Building had built into it an electric lift to the top storey. The telephone came into use after the Civil War and, after its invention in 1878, electric light became an essential feature, because, with the increasing height of buildings, came greater gloom for the lower floors. It was found that over about twenty-one metres (seventy feet), opening windows were impractical, because of the effects of the wind; so American engineers created the technology of air-conditioning. The steel frameworks themselves only became economic in the USA after the introduction by Andrew Carnegie (1835–1918) of the Bessemer process at Pittsburgh in the late 1860s, on a huge scale and at greatly-reduced cost.

Britain's centres and their development

The British ignored many of these new techniques, feeling secure in late-Victorian prosperity and confident of their ability to produce the best of everything. They changed their ideas very slowly, and were often over-cautious. The Ritz Hotel (1904), Britain's first major steel-framed building, also had load-bearing walls so as to be doubly sure that it would not collapse. Gradually the use of the new techniques and materials began and, with the introduction, on a wide scale, of the tower crane in the 1950s which brought down the cost of high-rise construction, high-rise building became a feature of nearly all modern urban areas of moderate size. Tower blocks became the biggest feature of the skyline. However, the collapse of the block at Ronan Point, in London, put a final nail in the coffin of their use for housing. They had already gone through a very disturbed social history, full of tales of the loneliness of tenants and vandalism. Few people lived in the high-rise, city-centre developments so that, in these cases, increasing height was an acceptable response to the rocketing price of land. As an example of the cost of prime development land, the Euston

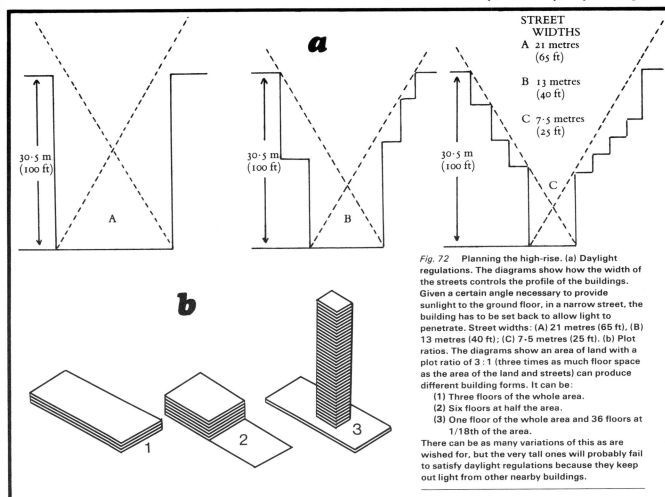

STREET
WIDTHS
A 21 metres
(65 ft)

B 13 metres
(40 ft)

C 7·5 metres
(25 ft)

Fig. 72   Planning the high-rise. (a) Daylight regulations. The diagrams show how the width of the streets controls the profile of the buildings. Given a certain angle necessary to provide sunlight to the ground floor, in a narrow street, the building has to be set back to allow light to penetrate. Street widths: (A) 21 metres (65 ft), (B) 13 metres (40 ft); (C) 7·5 metres (25 ft). (b) Plot ratios. The diagrams show an area of land with a plot ratio of 3 : 1 (three times as much floor space as the area of the land and streets) can produce different building forms. It can be:

(1) Three floors of the whole area.
(2) Six floors at half the area.
(3) One floor of the whole area and 36 floors at 1/18th of the area.

There can be as many variations of this as are wished for, but the very tall ones will probably fail to satisfy daylight regulations because they keep out light from other nearby buildings.

Centre complex, in central London, was built on land which cost £500,000 per acre (£1·2m per hectare). With land so expensive it had to be used to the greatest financial advantage.

Constant demolition and rebuilding, making more economic use of the land, swallowed up large areas of Victorian offices which had been restricted in their vertical growth by fire regulations. As we saw in study seven, these regulations are no longer effective in limiting the height of modern buildings. The controlling factor in the planning of new building is the attitude of local authorities and central planners to the use of the centre and the maximum height which should be allowed. Two measures of use and height were and are involved, the floor-space index and the plot ratio. In these the total floor area of the building is controlled according to the ground-floor area. Figure 72 shows how variations in design can produce different forms of building. The stepped profiles come about because, without the setting-back of the towers, there would be no daylight received at low levels. The floor-space index and plot ratio principle is operated by most local authorities to

control the upward growth of their centres. Sometimes it has been less than successful. A loophole in the 1947 Town and Country Planning Act allowed the enlargement of buildings by up to ten per cent of their cubic capacity. The large Victorian offices, with high ceilings, had large cubic capacities, but a limited number of floors. By demolishing them, and replacing them with modern structures, with low ceilings, it was possible to provide many more offices than the planners intended. Sometimes, the floor-space index became twice as large as the intended limit.

The high-rise feature is one of the most obvious physical characteristics of large urban centres. The present developments, built either of a steel frame with a skin of glass and aluminium, or of reinforced concrete, are likely to be temporary aspects of the urban landscape. Lacking the massive character of Victorian offices, they can be regarded as disposable units, ready for demolition and replacement when they become obsolete.

Not all buildings in the centres are high-rise; in some cases, it would be a positive disadvantage if they were. Shopping complexes are a good example.

In medieval towns, craftsmen displayed and sold their produce within their own houses. In some of them, the goods might be displayed in the windows, but these were very small. Later, window shutters were built which dropped down on chains to form a shelf from which goods could be sold. As the range of products offered to the public became larger and more sophisticated, so the method of retailing changed. As more outlets appeared, giving a greater and greater choice of products, customers tended to make more comparisons from shop to shop before buying. One of the major attractions of the city centre is the wide range of shops which sell these "comparison" goods. This choice is not available in suburban areas and smaller settlements. The greater range of these retail outlets does generate its own particular contribution to the urban landscape.

Walking around shopping areas is a visual experience. On all sides goods are displayed as attractively as possible, display being the important word. As retail specialization has increased, and the range of similar goods has grown, so easy access to the shopper and the roles of advertisement and display have become critical. Competition from other outlets together with the importance of "impulse buying" means that shops in the Central Area became keen rivals for the attention of passers-by. Some streets, because of their size, or their nearness to stations, car parks or bus routes, have greater advantages than others. They find it easier to assemble potential customers. To them come the shops,

Above: Fig. 73 **Controlled high-rise. New offices with a low-level base and a set-back tower. Referring back to windows and ventilation, this building integrated controls providing a constant internal "climate". No opening windows here.**

Below: Fig. 74 **A typical shopping area. The plan shows a real situation. The specializations are very limited, confined almost entirely to comparison goods. Each shop marked * belongs to a well-known national chain, appearing in almost all shopping centres. The best examples would be Woolworth's, Burton's and Marks and Spencer. Notice the use of arcades, to increase the display area, and of canopies, to protect shoppers while they gaze at the goods on show.**

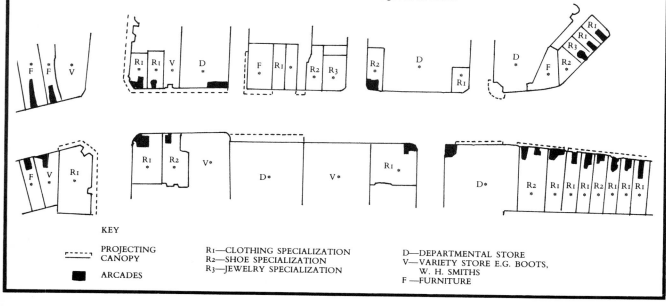

KEY

- - - - - PROJECTING CANOPY

⬛ ARCADES

R₁—CLOTHING SPECIALIZATION
R₂—SHOE SPECIALIZATION
R₃—JEWELRY SPECIALIZATION

D—DEPARTMENTAL STORE
V—VARIETY STORE E.G. BOOTS, W. H. SMITHS
F—FURNITURE

Above: Fig. 75   Victorian shops. This one is elegant and marked by a restraint in its advertising which contrasts with modern competitors.

Below: Fig. 76   **Town-centre shopping. The character of this area** is the same all over Britain, lots of lights, and sometimes music to draw in the casual shopper and tempt him or her to spend money. Above the ground floor, casual shopping becomes less convenient and less common.

Above: Fig. 77 Pedestrian areas. Most towns have a section of their shopping area in a pedestrianized, traffic-free arrangement. Sometimes they have precincts where shops are gathered together. This photograph shows a street recently converted to pedestrian principles. Notice how most people still walk along the old pavement sections. The arcades mentioned in the text can be seen well.

competing for the limited space, and sorting themselves into those who can afford high rents, and those who cannot. Those that can are the boutiques and shoe shops, the camera and fur stores, the jewellers and furnishers. There is a limited amount of street frontage and a limited amount of display area. The ground floor is the prime target for development, as most shoppers cannot see the first floor and above. Shops with large products, such as furniture, need large window areas, whereas jewellers can use small spaces. The demand for display area is so great that, if the street-front area of the shop is small, arcades may be built, corridors of temptation bringing the customers to the shop itself. Away from the main streets the shops change in character. Prime sites rely on attracting "impulse buyers" and window shoppers. Those away from the path of these casual customers must rely on supplying special necessities in order to draw people. So, in these positions, there are

sports goods, car accessory shops and do-it-yourself centres.

There are exceptions to the concentration on ground-floor locations. Department stores include within one building an amalgamation of many, specialist, comparison shops. They have ground-floor access, but the upper floors have no easy accessibility; so the modern department store depends on its elevators and escalators to ferry potential customers upstairs. Just as the land use changes outward from the main street, so it does with vertical movement. On the ground floor are the perfumes, cosmetics and haberdashery, bringing in the lunch-time office girls. The top floors are filled with carpets and furniture, accounts departments, restaurants and hairdressers. Most of these are goods and services for which shoppers make planned visits. The department store principle has, in the last thirty years, been followed by the shopping precinct, not one store with many departments, but one building with many stores. Once again, ease of movement is essential to the prosperity of the shops and the highest rents are paid by those which are nearest to the escalators or the car park access. During the same period, the pedestrianization of shopping areas, sometimes called precincting, has changed the whole character of Central Area retailing.

Study 10 The growth of advertising

Pawnbrokers and pubs

The medieval shop rarely needed an advertisement; often its product was very obvious. For example, the butchers would often do their slaughtering and carving in the streets, and the mounds of offal and streams of blood were an easy means of recognition. However, certain trades and professions adopted special signs to hang outside their premises. Some of these signs are still used today. The population of Britain was still largely illiterate, a condition which lasted well into the nineteenth century, and so there was little point in lengthy, written displays. The sign or symbol was the response to the situation; the longest-lasting examples are those of the pawnbroker's three golden balls and the barber's red and white striped pole. The former comes from the symbol used by the famous medieval banking family of the Lombards and the latter from the dual function of the barber in medieval times. As well as shaving, he was unofficial surgeon and blood-letter, hence the colour scheme, red for blood and white for the towels to mop it up with. We still use signs and symbols in our advertisements, although we almost always use words with them now. Some nineteenth-century signs have had words added to them later.

Public houses include some of the best examples of advertisements; almost every one has a picture as well as a name. Originally, medieval ale-houses had a trade sign, the alestake, a simple pole jutting out from the side of the building. They were forced to show this as a sign that they required (by law) the services of the aletaster, an official who supervised the price and quality of the product. If they were allowed to serve wine as well as ale, the alestake carried an evergreen bush on it. As more ale-houses opened, they began to hang signs on their alestakes. In this way they could acquire a reputation associated with a particular name. The signs were simple, easily-recognizable symbols, such as the sun, moon, plough, bull or crown, objects familiar to a population with little experience outside their own local area. Even today, although they combine words with the pictures, our public houses still include large numbers of *Brown Cows* and *Coach and Horses*, sometimes true descendants of the simple displays of hundreds of years ago.

Uses and abuses in the nineteenth century

In the last century, the bill-sticker and the fly-poster became common sights in towns and cities as more people were able to read and a bigger variety of goods and attractions appeared. In the centres, retailers tried to out-do each other with outrageous, often entirely false claims for their products. Advertising on hoardings became common after the 1850s and shops flew flags and balloons with the name of their specialization. Shop owners began to plaster their

---

Below: Fig. 78   **Pub displays. Victorian public houses show an enormous variety of decoration and display. This one, which may have changed its name, adds to its attractions with a roll-call of carved busts of Victorian authors.**

fronts with information. There were no controls on the amount of display, its content, or how it was organized. Often the hoardings themselves were dangerous, and in 1891 a number of people were injured when one blew down in Hyde Park.

Partly as a result of this, the London Sky Sign Act was passed in 1891, restricting unsightly hoardings and also balloons and flags. At this time, the lack of any control over the content of the advertisements allowed a wide range of approaches, including calculated lies and "suggestive" material, which outraged many Victorians. Some of the complaints were, by today's standards, laughable. Bovril, for example, was widely advertised using the figure of a bull. In Cork, the advertisement was objected to, on the grounds that it was likely to corrupt the morals of the young people of the town. Presumably, a neutered version would have been acceptable. An Indecent Avertisements Act was passed in 1889 and the Society for Checking the Abuse of Public Advertising was formed in 1893. Gradually controls began to be placed on the visual aspects of display, the pioneer piece of legislation being the Advertisement Regulation Act of 1907. This began the process of checking the intrusion of advertising into natural amenities, and also into the quality of the townscape. This has been a problem which has grown consistently for centuries. The pub sign, mentioned previously, had been one of the chief nuisances and, in London, they had been limited much earlier because they were so large that they blocked out sunlight in narrow streets.

Modern features and their control

The effects of progressive control can be seen in our central zones. The 1971 Town and Country Planning Act, for example, includes further provisions for "regulating the dimensions, appearance and position of advertisements which may be displayed, the sites on which advertisements may be displayed and the manner in which they are to be affixed". The controls apply to any display, *including* name plates, road traffic signs and even church notice boards, although the more innocent of them, such as business name plates, are usually automatically excluded from rigid control. The regulations have tended to standardize display, so that shop names are of the same dimensions, and the illuminated signs which protrude from so many buildings seem to have all come from the same mould. The extent of the Regulations is far-reaching, even extending to the price and information labels in shop windows, unless they are less than 0.1 square metres in area. But control only operates in the realms of public safety and amenity. The Regulations say nothing about the economic value or social desirability of advertising! They contain no prohibition on obscenity, or on the truthfulness of the content. Other laws deal with these. Few advertisers would risk prosecution for publishing obscene material, while the wild claims of nineteenth-century displays have disappeared in the face of legislation such as the Trades Descriptions Acts of 1968 and 1972. Since then, the number of posters boasting of "huge reductions" and "everything half-price" has tended to drop to very low levels.

Pictorial advertisement. Below: Fig. 79 **A bootmaker, probably adding the title after the boot and maker's name.** *Right top: Fig. 80* **An old brewery, the Elephant, converted to a pub and restaurant.** *Right bottom: Fig. 81* **Doorway to a long-gone smithy.**

Chapter 11 Postscript: reversing the trend

In the past, as British urban areas have grown, there has been a tendency for a greater and greater retail concentration in the centre. All over the residential areas, small family "convenience" shops became the normal pattern, as the high-quality, specialized sales gravitated to the Central Area. The last twenty years have seen this trend slow down, and in some places move gradually into reverse. The problems of the centres in terms of congestion, noise and parking difficulties have begun to make other patterns of shopping more attractive. From America, via Europe, we now have the hypermarket, a large integrated department-type store, but up-dated to deal with the demands of modern shoppers. Instead of a series of levels, there is only one and parking is provided for hundreds of cars. This organization demands greater space than the town-centre precinct. Hypermarkets are located mainly on land outside the urban boundaries. There are also more and more neighbourhood centres, district shopping centres, and suburban shops being built, especially where they can cope with the parking of customers' cars. All these trends tend to weaken the power of the core area. Table X shows the share of retail trade gained by the various types of shop. The department store, the central shop *par excellence*, has stagnated. The concentration of trade within the multiple stores is marked, taking away business from the independent shopkeeper, particularly the old corner-shop.

Guide to further study (for chapters ten and eleven)

These two chapters are combined because they and the studies with them revolve around the theme of planning. There is a large bibliography on this topic. A selection could be

The New Citizen's Guide to Town and Country Planning (Town and Country Planning Association, 1966)

W. Ashworth, *The Genesis of Modern British Town Planning* (Routledge, 1954)

G. E. Cherry, *The Evolution of British Town Planning* (Leonard Hill, 1974)

G. E. Cherry, *Urban Change and Planning. A History of Urban Development in Britain since 1750* (Foulis, 1972)

P. Hall, *Urban & Regional Planning* (David & Charles, 1975/Penguin, 1975)

J. Holliday (ed), *City Centre Redevelopment* (Charles Knight, 1974) for accounts of the policy in larger cities

J. B. Cullingworth, *Town and Country Planning in Britain* (Allen & Unwin, 1972)

Urban sprawl can be studied from maps. Small-scale maps are useful here. Take an early 1:63,360 (one inch to a mile) and find the total urbanized area by counting the squares of the kilometre grid. Repeat the exercise for a modern map

Below: Table X   A multiple shop is one belonging to a retailing organization which has ten or more branches.

As a result of the decline in the power of the small independent shop, the number of shops in Britain is expected to decline from 542,000 in 1961 to 450,000 in 1975.

The share of retail trade of various shop types Percentage share of total trade in			
Type of shop	1957	1966	1975 (estimated)
Department stores	5	5	5
Multiple shops	24	32	39·5
Cooperatives	12	9	8
Independent	57	50	41·5
(Mail order	2	4	6)

and then compare the increase in the area with the increase in the population of the urban area. Area will in all cases increase much more rapidly than the number of people. Maps of this scale from the 1930s show ribbon development very well.

For the town or city centre information on functions comes from Yellow Pages and other directories. It is possible to use the rateable values of buildings as measures of their importance and local rate books are available at the town hall or council offices. Local authorities will also have information on the type of legislation they use in the planning of building height, for example the plot ratio they employ. On the growth of tall buildings see

C. Condit, *The Rise of the Sky-scraper* (Cambridge University Press, 1952)

Direct recording provides most information from this area. Surveys of the height of buildings can be used for cross-sections of the Central Area to illustrate the relationship between centrality and tall buildings. Surveys of the location of particular shops and offices can be used in two dimensions. For example how do shop types vary with increasing distance from A the main roads and B from the ground floor. How do shop types relate to each other? For example, it is surprising how frequently shoe shops are next to dress shops. Methods of measuring this adjacency are in

D. P. Chappalaz & others, *Hypothesis testing in Field Studies* (Geographical Association, 1970)

Yellow Pages and directories can be used for comparing the shopping areas of different towns examining how frequently the same national names recur.

There is so much information available that it is often a problem to decide What is important? or What can I do with it if I collect it? Standard works on methods of collection and techniques of analysis are

G. B. G. Bull, *A Town Study Companion* (Hulton, 1973)
H. Cross & P. Daniel, *Fieldwork for Geography Classes* (McGraw-Hill, 1968)
K. Briggs, *Fieldwork in Urban Geography* (Oliver & Boyd, 1971)
J. Haddon, *Local Geography in Towns* (Philip, 1971)

More advanced techniques of quantitative analysis come in

P. Toyne & P. T. Newby, *Techniques in Human Geography* (Macmillan, 1971)
W. V. Tidswell & S. M. Barker, *Quantitative Methods* (University Tutorial Press, 1971)
W. H. Theakstone & C. Harrison, *The Analysis of Geographical Data* (Heinemann, 1970)
P. McCullagh, *Data use and interpretation* (Oxford University Press, 1974)

There is also another standard text on urban study already referred to (study guide, chapter two), which does not fit easily into any of the separate bibliographies. This is

J. A. Everson & B. P. Fitzgerald, *Inside the City* (Longman, 1972)

which deals with urban models, land use, the pattern of business centres and shopping centres, fields of influence, housing and social change, commuting and New Towns. It deals not only with theory but with methods of analysis and is highly recommended.

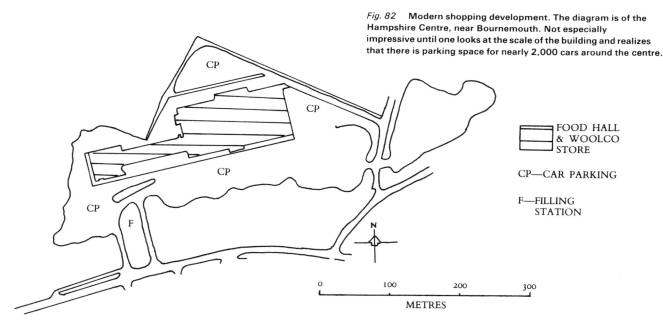

Fig. 82 **Modern shopping development. The diagram is of the Hampshire Centre, near Bournemouth. Not especially impressive until one looks at the scale of the building and realizes that there is parking space for nearly 2,000 cars around the centre.**

FOOD HALL & WOOLCO STORE

CP—CAR PARKING

F—FILLING STATION

12 Preserving the past

Although the Central Area is dominated by buildings organized for profit, they do not make up the total land-use of the zone. Most of our urban developments have grown slowly, relative to the rate of growth of those in North America. Ours therefore had time to build up a legacy of buildings from previous eras, buildings which have not been entirely erased, and have developed uses unrelated to profit. There *are* British towns which mushroomed into a type of instant urbanization, such as Oldham and Middlesbrough, but the majority began with a medieval foundation and expanded from it. Within the original structure of the town some buildings developed particular distinction and value because of their service to the community as a whole. The best examples are churches and castles which in many cases formed the focal point from which the urban area grew. With an increase in the power of local administration, particularly after 1835 when the growing townships of the Industrial Revolution were able to apply for municipal status, the town hall became a frequent building of note. The nineteenth century was responsible for most of the public buildings we have now. New urban centres erected museums, libraries and concert halls, as well as town halls, often producing grandiose schemes to reflect their new economic power. In the large industrial towns, new growth often replaced older structures as the demand for land increased. So, in the larger conurbations, with the exception of London, the historical range of buildings is almost totally compressed into the last hundred and fifty years.

The nineteenth-century, central buildings were on a grand scale. Depending on the tastes of the council, they were either neo-Classical, or Gothic Revival. Replicas of Greek and Roman temples spread across the country, side-by-side with turrets and spires copied from Gothic cathedrals. The most famous public building in Britain, the Houses of Parliament, ushered in the main wave of the Gothic. As both the centres and the urban areas grew, so the councils became more powerful, and their buildings more imposing. By the end of the century, councils had more power over local fortunes than they had ever had before. This power ensured that the public buildings themselves became protected sections of the built environment, safe except for changes brought about by the councils themselves. While all around them Victorian commercial premises were constantly being demolished and replaced, they remained and in most cases we still have the original structures. In the case of private buildings, there were few checks on demolition and redevelopment. Most councils were proud of the rapid changes taking place and were more concerned with looking forward rather than

Fig. 83 The town needs planning. Here although the buildings in the foreground are protected, they are overwhelmed by the ones at the rear of them. It can be arranged that new developments blend with the old; notice the careful way the offices on the extreme right have been designed.

backward. Official conservation of areas and buildings has been very much a twentieth-century practice. The only exceptions have been churches. In the past, especially in Victorian times, they were more publicly used and greater public concern was expressed about their fate, but nowadays many of them remain in parts of the city where the population has moved out to new housing estates. Standing alone and little used, they are an easy prey for vandals, and church authorities are forced to have them closed up or pulled down.

The commercial centres are in a constant state of turmoil. Particular buildings become too small or are ill-designed for new purposes and so they are replaced by others. Every centre has its sections where haulage contractors are carting away the remnants of old buildings and where, within a few months, they will be replaced by new ones. Throughout the ravages brought about by commercial redevelopment of town centres, most public buildings have remained standing. If the British had a system where the value of land in the centres was measured and decisions taken on purely financial grounds, then they would have long since vanished. Town centres in Britain would display the

American pattern. That they do not is due, not to some inherent British love for historic architecture, but to the long history of building styles, which have not yet been eliminated in the urban areas.

Conservation and preservation of buildings is now commonplace in this country. Slowly, over the last hundred years, it has been realized that there is a need to retain buildings from the past, even when their usefulness seems to have disappeared. One obvious reason for preserving them arises from the fact that they are often more attractive than modern designs. Most people are able to appreciate the style and grace of Georgian squares and crescents or the beauty of a village made up of old thatched cottages. However, they are also important because they help us to understand aspects of life in the past. Many "stately homes", kept alive by income from visitors, are objects of historical interest, showing the life-style of past nobility. In a less romantic sphere, we are also preserving old workhouses, schools, factories and railway stations. Conservation and preservation cost money and it also needs strong organization as there are often sound commercial reasons for pulling down an old building and replacing it with a more

Below: Fig. 84 **Is this preservation? The building being redeveloped was early nineteenth-century Classical. The front has been retained because of listing as a classified building, but everything else has been carted away.**

Above: Fig. 85   **Worth saving? This arrangement dating from medieval organization is not the most efficient imaginable. It could be demolished if there were no powers to control how the environment is developed.**

efficient modern structure. The authority which is to regulate these changes must be a strong one, capable of refusing even the most powerful developer and the main responsibility for protecting the built environment now rests with local and national government. Over the last fifty years they have built up our controls relating to development, so that there are now well-established codes of practice for protecting buildings.

The Department of the Environment is able to list individual, or groups of, buildings as being of "special architectural or historic interest". They are graded 1, 2 or 3 depending on how important they are considered to be. Age is an important factor in determining whether a building or area should be listed. All buildings of before 1700, which survive in anything like their original condition, are listed, as are most between 1700 and 1840. Those between 1840 and 1914 are selected for their quality and character, to include examples of the social and economic life of the time, such as markets, schools and prisons. At the end of 1974 there were 207,000 classified buildings in England and Wales. They are graded 1, 2*, 2 or 3, according to how important the Inspectors of the Department of the Environment consider them to be. Grade 1 buildings are not common and they cannot be altered, even by the owners, without the Department's permission. Grades 2*, 2 or 3 apply to less important features but they also have restrictions on how they may be altered. Theirs are less strict than those of Grade 1 but they cannot be demolished without permission. Listing in Grades 2 and 3 has often been no obstacle to redevelopment by property owners and speculative builders. For someone wishing to build a valuable office block on the site of a listed building, the fine for illegal demolition, a maximum of £400 at present, is hardly likely to be much of a deterrent. The 1974 Town and Country Amenities Act provides the threat of prison for offenders but no one has yet been sentenced. However, fine buildings are becoming more secure, both because of planning restriction and because the public themselves are becoming more aware of the situation. European Architectural Heritage Year saw many towns and cities producing displays to show how they were conserving their historic buildings and much support was shown by members of the public. The planners who operate the system do make mistakes at times, but they are on most occasions helping to retain something of the individuality of the past within the box buildings of the present.

Towns in Britain display, not only past buildings, but other remnants which appear in more subtle forms. As the towns have changed over hundreds of years, they have often retained part of their original plan. When buildings fell down, or were demolished, they were usually rebuilt using the same building line in relation to the street. There was no need to replan or realign the street, but it had to be wide enough for the carriage and pedestrian traffic of the time. So, in many centres, the narrow streets of the sixteenth and seventeenth centuries remain. It may be, of course, that the street has been altered, but even if its dimensions are different, it usually retains its old name. A study of these names, and their association with past features and functions, is a useful method of assessing the influence of the past upon the present.

Guide to further study

Source books on street names are sections of:
K. Cameron, *English Place Names* (Methuen, 1959, 3 vols)
G. J. Copley, *English Place Names and their Origin* (David & Charles, 1971)

Local authorities have information on listed buildings and Conservation Areas within their districts. Go and see why they should be preserved. Are there any omissions from the list? If you know of buildings of special character you should inform the local authority especially if there is a possibility of their destruction. Information (dates of construction, features and evaluation of importance) on the major buildings of particular areas in England is available in the appropriate volume of the Buildings of England series by Sir Nikolaus Pevsner, published by Penguin Books on a county basis.

Personal research dealing with change will probably involve the use of historical sources but more should be done to record *present* environments by surveys and photographs. Urban areas change so rapidly that any work soon becomes of historical interest.

Study 11 Street names as a guide to the past

The Romans began the process of naming streets within Britain, but the practice has not been continuously observed throughout the period since. The naming of every passage, alley and lane within urban areas is comparatively recent; it was only by the 1875 Public Health Act that councils were expected to give them a formal identification. In medieval towns, small lanes might become known after the person who lived there, or whose house lay at its end, but it was only the major thoroughfare which received a formal title. The chief one was normally named High Street, or Fore Street. If the latter, then behind it would be Back Street. Similarly, one could have Higher and Lower, and Upper and Nether. In the Midlands and North of England, "gate" was often used instead of "street", derived from the Norse *gata*, meaning way, or path. Other streets would often include reference to particular buildings such as Church Street, or pay homage to local nobility, either as plain Lord Street, or by including the name of the particular member of the gentry.

Functional names

As the towns grew, they acquired market functions. Sometimes they are located by Market Street itself, although this can cover a wide range of time, through to the twentieth century. Of greater interest are the special-produce markets, remaining as Cattle, Butter, Horse and Haymarkets. Again, the last two served an important function into this century, when horses were as common as cars. Sometimes the original form of the specialized product is confusing, as in the Bigg (barley) Market in Newcastle, or the Madder (a material used in dyeing) Market in Norwich. Together with the suffix "-market" as an area for retailing, we have "-fair", as in Horsefair Street (Leicester), or the assocation with a cross, as in Poultry Cross (Salisbury), showing where selling was concentrated. Other words which refer to marketing include the widespread Cheap-, or Chipping, from the Old English *cēap* and *cēping*.

With the development of specialized trades within the towns, there often occurred a concentration of crafts and skills into one area. The Fleshshambles was the common street name for a row of slaughterers, remaining notably in the Shambles of York. The butchers were alternatively called fleshers and in places this remains in a changed form, as in Fletcher Gate in Nottingham. Along with the butchers would be the seasoners, selling spices to add to over-ripe meat. If there were a number of them, they might produce a Pepper Street. Fisher, used with Lane, Gate or Street, does not always indicate fishermen, but could refer to the area where dried, salt fish were sold. Saltergate is another

example of a name having grown from a specific function and the processing of agricultural goods would give Bread Street and Bakehouse Street.

Manufacturing could be similarly concentrated. Tanner, Saddler, Wheelmaker, Smith and Ironmonger are obvious clues where they appear before a street or lane. Others which may have an early origin, include Mercer (silk trader), Lister (dyers) and Hosier, all from the textile trades. Nottingham has a fine selection of old street names, including Pilcher Gate (the making of outer garments), Barker Gate (tanners), Carter Gate (skins) and The Drapery, where cloth was made. Figure 86 is a plan of the present streets of the centre of Nottingham, and from it can be seen the significance of the relic name pattern. Among local street names derived from trades, there may be some which we might not recognize today. So there is Billiter Street in London, derived from the bell-founders, Paternoster Street, "the street of the makers of rosaries", Skeldergate in York from the shield-makers and Waterbeer Street in Exeter, where the water-carriers met, or lived.

Descriptive names

Not every street would have some specific function which was concentrated within it and often the name would evolve from some other conspicuous feature of the environment. Outside streets, which might be cobbled, most of the passages would be unpaved and, during wet weather, would degenerate into small rivers and areas of ankle-deep mud. In the poorer parts of the town, the housing was of the same standard of attraction. Paradise Steet was a relatively common name, and it was not intended to be complimentary. Rotten Row meant "rat row" and other expressions implying poor quality were Wet Lane, Stinking Lane, Full ("foul") Street, and Summer Lane, which was usable only during the summer. Streets in good condition, perhaps in areas of higher-order housing, could show themselves in Broad-, for their dimensions, or Pavement (York and Nottingham) for their material. Particular ethnic groups might give an area a special character, more so if they were easily recognized by their language or religion. Thus, there is Lombard Street, Danesgate, Flemingate and a host of names associated with Jews, such as Old Jewry in London, and Jury Street in Warwick.

As the towns grew, the number of specialized buildings and areas increased. The names still with us are sometimes a useful guide to the important building in past lay-outs. Castle Street is a widespread example, with Well Street and Mill Street being common elements in urban names. Church Street also appears as Kirkgate, Spital Street refers

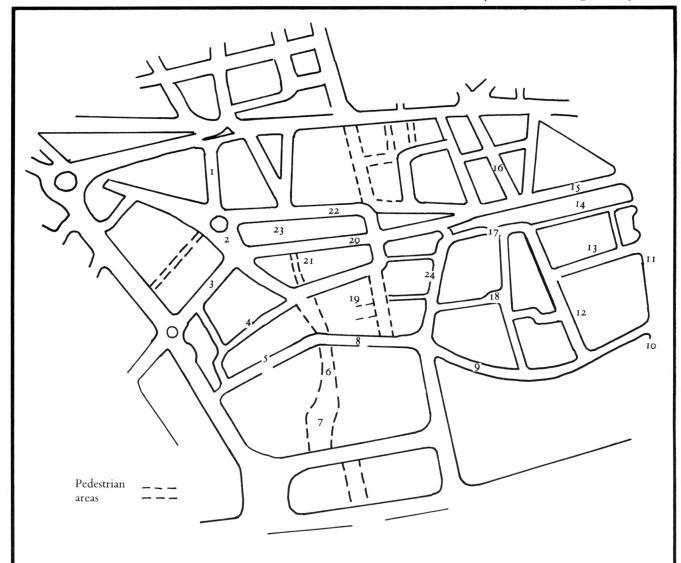

Key to Nottingham street map (Fig. 86)

1. Market Street
2. Beastmarket
3. Friary Lane
4. Hounds Gate
5. Castle Gate
6. Listergate
7. Greyfriar Gate
8. Lower Pavement
9. High Pavement
10. Fishergate
11. Bellar Gate
12. Stoney Street
13. Barker Gate
14. Woolpack Lane
15. Goose Gate
16. Broad Street
17. Warser Gate
18. Pilcher Gate
19. Pepper Street
20. Cheapside
21. Exchange Walk
22. Smithy Row
23. Old Market Square
24. Fletcher Gate

Above: Fig. 87   **An industrial name. This nineteenth-century mill was almost certainly patriotically named after Napoleon's place of exile.**

to the medieval "hospital" and, in the eighteenth and nineteenth centuries, Union Street referred to the workhouse of the Poor Law Union. Pillory Lane occurs in London and Gallowgate in Newcastle. With physical expansion, New and Newlands Street mark where the boundaries of the existing township were extended, often into previously-cultivated farmland. For this reason, farm names appear in many urban areas, and can be used in reconstruction. Field descriptions such as Long Meadow are common, and others involve comments on the character of the land, such as Marsh Lane, or Rocky Lane.

A change in approach. Less reality, but more precise dating

However, there comes a time in the growth of any particular urban area when these indicators need to be treated with caution. Many modern suburban names are concocted, less with a view to description of the actual environment, than to the public relations principle that a pretty name is half-way towards making a pretty environment. We therefore have an abundance of titles which do not bear any relationship to the character of the district. Real examples of this type can be found in any suburban district, Rosefields, Greenhills and Woodviews and others, having no connection with roses, green hills or woods.

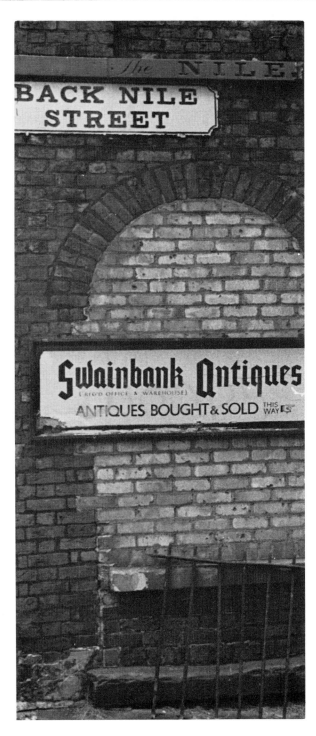

Above: Fig. 88   **Nineteenth-century tavern. Built soon after Nelson's victory in Egypt, the bricked-up window may have been the "jug and bottle", the off-licence of the time. The name cut in the stone refers to the tavern, which gave its name to the street, sometime later.**

From the nineteenth century onward, the naming of roads becomes a more official function, and the days when a name grew out of its surroundings became less frequent. Increasingly names began to reflect the political, economic and social attitudes and events which were occurring when the area was built up. Estate developers, whether of the sophisticated crescents and squares of Belgravia, or the tenements of the industrial towns, used the names of the aristocracy and royalty, popular political figures and famous historical events. Especially in middle- and low-income housing, which was generally built in extensive areas within a short period, there is a marked uniformity about the names. Prime Minister follows Prime Minister and one county name appears after another. The chief interest in this attitude to naming comes from the use of contemporary events as sources, and the use which can be made of them. After particular wars, whole districts were decorated with the more notable of the victories, or the generals. After the Crimea, Sebastopol and Inkerman became part of every industrial town and city, as previously Waterloo had done. No self-respecting unit would fail to have some monument to Wellington and Nelson, sometimes naming the entire town after one of them. The value of these names lies in the fact that there was seldom a gap of more than ten years from the date of the event to the outbreak of the derived street names. Therefore, it is possible to use specific names as a guide to dating in urban environments. Politicians, royalty and their jubilees, authors and military exploits are all good examples. Unfortunately, the growth in the number of streets usually exceeded the supply of patriotic names, and so much of the working-class housing is reduced to long lists of obscure plants or trees, or a full roll-call of biblical characters. It is difficult to use these as evidence of anything but the sheer rate of growth, although the casts from the works of specific authors, such as Dickens, tell us *after* which date the streets were built.

In the twentieth century we have changed our approach once more. Perhaps our politicians seem to be less worthy of remembrance, and we may be less jingoistic about success in battle. Certainly we cannot expect to find every Prime Minister of this century commemorated in each urban area. Kitchener, Haig and Montgomery are no competition to Wellington. A more subdued phraseology develops, more generally descriptive, like the suburban ones which hopefully hint at the charms and delights of their surroundings. There are some exceptional individuals, like Churchill and John F. Kennedy, who are almost obligatory members of city directories but, unlike our ancestors, we are not leaving behind many clues for future investigators.

13 The outer areas – suburban housing

Outside the Central Area lies the main body of the urban region, both in terms of population and area. Referring back to the ideas contained within chapter two, and in particular to the concentric approach, we can in many cases see the zonation of residential and other use as we move from the centre. The zones are not always as clear-cut and precise as we might hope for, but the broad outlines are there in every town of moderate size. In the model, the inner zones are occupied mainly by low-income housing, which is succeeded by more expensive homes as we move outward. In most urban areas in Britain this theoretical pattern is disturbed. There is no automatic separation of social and income groups as is implied in the model. For example, in theory, the outer-suburban perimeter should be occupied by families which have a "white-collar" executive as the head of the household, two cars and a higher than average income. However, because of political and social factors, we have a situation where the outer zone is often one of local authority housing, often rehousing, in large estates where the incomes are certainly not the highest in the community. Local authority housing does not confine itself to any particular section of the urban framework. It therefore distorts the model which we have taken from North American experience. Nevertheless we do have broad bands where differences are visible; in many cases, it *is* an historical process and a movement outward gives a panorama of the changes which have taken place over the last hundred and fifty years. In particular, it illustrates the changing views which society has had on the character of urban development.

Immediately outside the Central Area is a section of no-man's-land called in North America, the Transition Zone. It does not have the accessibility of the centre, and therefore, does not become host to the specialist retail and commercial interests. However, it is near enough to act as a supplier and so it has become the main area for wholesalers and warehouses. Interspersed with these, are small factories, especially for clothing, and tiny workshops, such as those specializing in motor repairs. In the nineteenth century, this area was also densely populated. On the fringes of the original town centre, in the case of the industrial towns, it was built up during the first expansionary period. Here Georgian terraces housed the merchants and businessmen who were still, at that time, able to walk to their place of

work. With the continued expansion of the towns, they moved out to areas still largely rural, and their original houses became occupied by poorer families. Crammed together, a family to a room, they were joined by more of the poor as speculative builders built new courts and terraces. The housing in this zone has steadily become worse and worse, partly because of poor-quality construction, but also because of neglect. In general, it has been multi-occupied by the poor and by small, transitory firms, using the building for a short time and then moving away, or going bankrupt. In the USA this is the area of the ghettoes and "Skid Row", and in Britain the worst social conditions have usually been found in this zone, together with the headquarters of organized vice. Now, most of the houses

Below: Fig. 89 **Part of the Transition Zone. Nineteenth-century warehouses, partly timber-framed, unused and neglected until some use can be found for the land. (Demolished in 1975.)**

are going, or have gone, cleared by local authorities. If these areas are not rebuilt, then their major use becomes off-street parking. They are often desolate spaces, devastated by clearance, with the odd, old rickety building still standing and few people, seemingly without much of a definite future.

The size of the Transition Zone varies and in small towns there may be no more than a few streets which have its characteristics. In almost all cases it leads outward to low-income housing, dating from about 1850 at the earliest, with its bulk being post-1875, after the Act producing the regular bye-law landscape. Little, if anything, remains of the types which dominated the first stages of growth. The courts and the back-to-backs have disappeared in most areas, demolished to make way for improvements. This is an important point to recognize in the study of the urban landscape; we only see the best of the past periods, the remainder having fallen or been pulled down. Within the nineteenth-century housing are the meagre services which the poor attracted. There were no glossy shopping centres, as there were no parklands and play areas. The corner shop was, and still is, the main form of retail outlet. In the past, the function of the corner shop was to supply the everyday needs of the men and women living in the immediate vicinity. It gave out goods in small quantities and hoped that its customers would be able to clear their debts on pay-day.

The section below describes the trade of a corner shop in Salford during the early years of this century.

"The very poor never fell into debt: nobody allowed them any credit. Paying on the nail, they bought in minimal quantities, sending their children usually for half a loaf, a ha'p'orth of tea, sugar, milk or a scrap of mustard pickled cauliflower in the bottom of a jar. Generally, two ounces of meat or cheese was the smallest quantity one could buy; to sell less, shopkeepers said, was to lose what tiny profit they got through 'waste in cutting'. Yet poor folk would try again and again, begging for smaller amounts — 'Just a penn'orth o' cheese' — to fry with this two ounces of bacon.' My father would not deign to attend to any of these 'shipping orders', as he called them; an elder sister took indigent pence. 'It's all cash,' she said briskly. Nor would Lipton, or 'Sir Thomas', as my mother named him, have truck with any who tried to buy a single boot-lace or asked him to divorce a pair of kippers. Such things, he seemed to believe, came to man in natural pairs, binary as bosoms.''

Robert Roberts, *The Classic Slum*, 1971, pp. 80–1.

Now, the corner shop is less important for its customers who are richer and more mobile and who cover a wider area in their shopping. Such small shops cannot compete

Below: Fig. 90   **Almost down and almost out.**

Above: Fig. 91 **No cheer for the small corner-shop. They are dying out fast in competition with the multiple stores. This one is still open despite its appearance.**

with the supermarkets' cut prices. They survive only by staying open late at night and on Sundays, and perhaps because for some they have a social function as a place of personal service and local gossip. The other services in the zone of low-income housing are few and often official. The main breaks in the terraces come from the old Board schools, the workhouses which have become hospitals, and the churches, built to provide the spiritual help the poor were felt to be in need of. However, the aid the poor themselves sought was usually in ale and spirits, and the numerous public houses were probably the most important feature relieving their misery, even if they created as many social problems as they solved. The schools came to the area after it was realized that the poor could and should be educated. Except for the church schools, they mostly appear during and after the 1870s and the Education Act of 1875. The Workhouses were there to take in the old and

homeless, often accelerating their death. The churches, built at a rate and scale no other century could match, were the result of the Church Commissioners' desire to match church building with population growth. The Church Building Society was formed in 1818 and raised £4½ million by the 1830s towards the erection of new churches for the Church of England. Parliament gave £1½ million, and 214 churches were built, concentrated in the growing industrial towns. Incidentally, 174 of them were described as "Gothic in style". Roman Catholic churches appeared later, following the Irish immigrations of the late 1840s.

The most notable absentee from this part of the town is the open space. There is frequently a total absence of parks, playgrounds and playing-fields. The only places available for recreation are the remains of the cleared housing and the occasional small public garden, perhaps celebrating one of Queen Victoria's jubilees.

In the 1920s, when local authorities began building houses on a vast scale, the only areas which were available lay on the edge of the towns. The council-house lists, which decided who was to have one of the new homes, usually favoured large families. Previously, these might have lived with their parents-in-law in the family terrace, or shared

Above: Fig. 92 "Garden tenements" of the 1930s. It is hard to think of a description less appropriate.

rooms in rented property. As the young families moved out to the new estates, they left behind an ageing population. New residents moved in, but, wherever councils were powerful, the growth of suburban estates meant that the inner areas were continually losing their younger people. Some inner-area tenement housing was built, especially in the 1930s, but still the young drifted outwards. In some of our larger towns and cities, large sections of older housing were destroyed in the Second World War. A growing atmosphere of decay hung over the inner areas. However, the last twenty years have seen a change in attitude towards the inner areas, a process which normally operates under the name of "urban renewal".

After 1919, there had been an increasing recognition by the Government of the problems of slum housing. The large cities and conurbations were most involved because they had the greatest problem not only in terms of numbers, but also in their percentages of unfit housing. As a result, whole districts were flattened and the families rehoused, especially after the 1930 Housing Act which gave grants to local authorities for clearance and rehousing. Urban renewal came into being because of the problems which were created by demolition. Many of the nineteenth-century

Above: Fig. 92 "Garden tenements" of the 1930s. It is hard to think of a description less appropriate.

terraces were built at densities of over 125 houses to the hectare, and the courts would be at much greater concentrations. Unless their narrow streets, small rooms and tiny backyards were to be rebuilt, exactly replaced, then it would not be possible to rehouse the population in the same area, at least not in individual houses. Semi-detached housing, for example, was rarely at more than 30 to the hectare. If terraces at 125 to the hectare were demolished, and rebuilt at semi-density, then the inhabitants of 95 of the former houses would be homeless. The solution to this was usually a dual approach; part of the rehousing was in flats, built in the old district, and part was in the suburban estates. The flats of the 1930s and 1940s were not tower blocks, more large, barrack-like tenements, with concrete playing areas, often built, like the terraces, row after row. It was quite common for them to be called "gardens", although little trace of greenery was visible. Figure 92 shows a good example of this style and organization.

They were generally not popular, as they lacked the sense of community which the courts and terraces had, at least, provided. The same complaint was made by those forced to move out to the suburbs. They found themselves in new communities with few social benefits. Sometimes the shops, public houses and community centres arrived years after the first houses. In some suburban areas, Saturday night was a time when the adults went back home, back to the inner areas, where they could meet old friends and families, and where they could find the social facilities they needed. Since 1950, the character of inner area development has changed again. For much of the period since then, the tower block, up to twenty-five or thirty storeys, has become dominant. They came with a realization that the tenements were often no improvement on what they had replaced. One particular drawback was the lack of open spaces. These could be provided if the building height increased, and more land was made available. But larger buildings gave greater opportunity for vandalism and widely-spaced tall buildings often caused wind effects which made garden areas between them unusable. Problems of isolation, loneliness and lack of play space for young children have led to another change of direction, away from the high-rise and towards lower maisonettes and deck-dwellings.

All these changes have transformed the old, inner areas. Many of the developments have appeared because of new attitudes which are increasingly dominating the planning of our towns and cities. In the nineteenth century, for most of the population, their surroundings mattered little. For most of them life centred around work and sleep. In this century, slowly it becomes accepted that urban areas should be organized so that all aspects of life are considered and made more pleasant. The town, or city, is not only a place to work in, but somewhere to live in every sense. The quality of that life depends, in many ways, on the planning of our surroundings, the organization of all we need to make life enjoyable. We have changed our views on this

Left: Fig. 94   **Modern, suburban local-authority planning. Typical of developments since the 1950s with a mixed high-rise and low-level arrangement. This releases some land for recreation but the problems of suburban estates and of high-rise living are sometimes combined.**

Guide to further study

Refer back to the appendix to chapters ten and eleven for the books on the development of planning. *Homes, Towns and Traffic* by Tetlow and Goss, published by Faber, 1970 (chapter four), is also useful.

Local authorities will have copies of the various Town Plans and Development Plans which they have been responsible for. They probably have models of their present hopes and larger towns mount permanent exhibitions in their planning offices. The same group probably have a special policy for the problems of their inner areas and pamphlets can be obtained cheaply.

The Development Corporation of a particular New Town will supply information on the aims of the development, its social, industrial and housing policy and progress so far. The maps are particularly useful.

Surveys of Transition Zones/Inner Areas are really only feasible in larger urban areas where the section is easily recognized. Observe and record such features as number and percentage of vacant or derelict buildings, the extent of cleared areas, the amount of off-street parking. In areas which maintain signs of life, up-to-date maps, whether Ordnance Survey or personal, are useful for ideas of housing density and amounts of recreational space. Compare it with either suburban estates or with areas of inner area "renewal". Visit renewal zones, examine their problems. Are they an improvement?

Many of the pioneer developments such as Bournville, Letchworth, Saltaire and Port Sunlight are situated in more densely-populated parts of the country. The best way of understanding them is to visit them. The same is true of the New Towns where guides are available to take parties around the area.

Publications of the Town and Country Planning Association are a useful addition to a library within this topic. Besides their periodical *Town and Country Planning Review* there is the *Bulletin of Environmental Education* or BEE. This is an excellent publication with lists of material for use within the city and suggestions for a variety of ways of looking at planning and the environment.

Bibliography:

See list in appendix to chapters ten and eleven plus

F. Schaffer, *The New Town Story* (MacGibbon and Kee, 1972)

H. Evans (ed), *New Towns: the British Experience* (T&CP Association, 1972)

organization, and we can trace the development over the last hundred and fifty years of an increasingly socially-directed view of planning.

Much of the legislation which has been passed in the nineteenth and twentieth centuries dealing with the environment has been to provide the less able sections of society with what they lacked through economic weakness. With regard to the ideas on better environments, the rich and powerful enjoyed their benefits long before the rest of the population. Gardens, parkland and low-density housing have been characteristic of their life-style for hundreds of years. Slowly, the higher standards have filtered down to the remainder of society. Much of the improvement has been due to political changes, such as the granting of the vote to all social groups. Political parties grew to represent the opinions and hopes of deprived groups and attitudes changed in society as a whole. Increasingly, people wish to see our society develop as an interrelated unit, one which has moved away from being an unequal contest between social groups. The changes have shown themselves in the urban landscape, where they gradually appear as new ideas on how urban areas should be arranged.

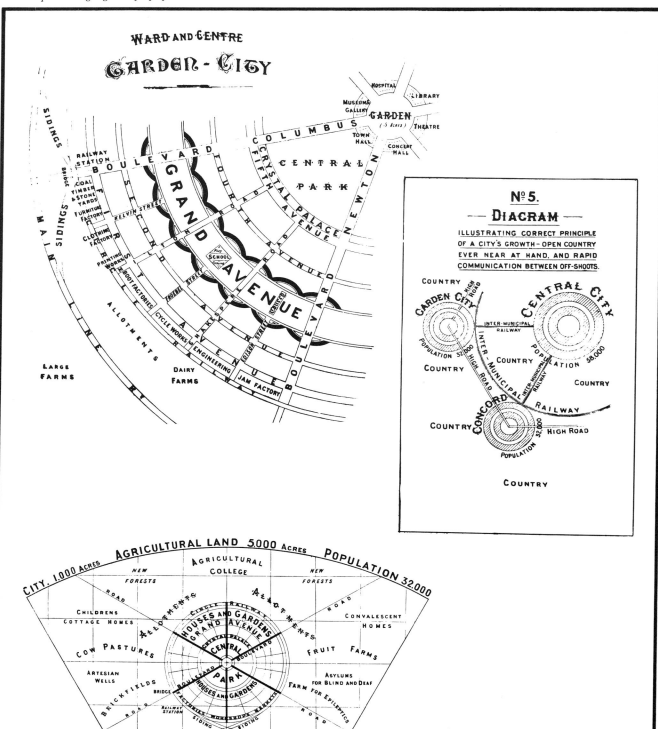

Fig. 95   Howard's diagrammatic "garden city", 1898.

Study 12 Designing towns for people

People's needs

We can take three main features to show how changing viewpoints have been reflected in environmental improvement. These are, firstly, the relationships between home, work and services — the town-dweller's need for employment, for family life and privacy, and for the services which can make material and social life more pleasant. Secondly, there are the demands for recreation and leisure, growing with greater affluence and shorter working periods. The third factor discussed is transport, concentrating especially on the problems which have grown because of the increasing numbers of cars. A natural desire for mobility and freedom has produced great environmental pressures. Most people tend to think of pressures on the countryside, but there are equal problems in towns and cities. Congestion and noise, injuries and death to pedestrians and drivers, pollution and demands for more road space are all at conflict with what might be expected to be the greatest good for all. In dealing with these three factors we will see that the changes and improvements interrelate at some times, and operate independently at others. Added together, the adaptations of design which they have caused produce much of our present urban organization. More importantly, they are shaping a greater proportion of our future.

As we have seen, in the last century economic forces were the final arbiter affecting the arrangement of the urban areas. In this system, the poor got low-quality housing and the rich high; services, both retail and commercial, gravitated to where they considered they could gain the maximum income. There were very few of the social services which we take for granted, because they are not profit-making, and there were no strong movements towards providing free facilities at that time. Gardens and parks were often viewed as commercial attractions, adding to the value of the adjacent property. Many parks were laid out as developments in which the high-quality housing around them was an essential section. There will, of course, always be variations within the urban landscape caused by economic factors, and many would say that an absolute uniformity would be undesirable. But, by the early Victorian period, it had become clear to some people that a system which relied entirely on "the survival of the richest" was not necessarily good for the country as a whole. Chadwick and the Public Health reformers set in motion the procedures for improving the minimum standards of environmental health, which had such a great effect on aspects of life as we have seen in study one.

However, the quality of housing was only one feature of individual lives. There are also work and recreation and all three of them interact. It was of small comfort that housing improved if, outside the home, conditions remained primitive, with work carried out in dirty cellars and with an almost total lack of space for play and leisure. For a large proportion of town dwellers in the nineteenth century, the whole urban environment was a depressing one. Yet it was not a necessary condition of urban life; the better-off lived in very adequate surroundings, the early part of the century seeing the development of gracious squares and crescents, often accompanied by their own private park. The contrast was only partly explained by wealth. A main cause of the problems of low-income areas was that few powerful figures saw any political or social necessity for them to champion the cause of the unfortunate inhabitants, and therefore little thought was given as to how these communities should be organized.

Ideas on social equality were increasingly voiced in the late eighteenth and early nineteenth centuries. The French Revolution increased interest in the lessening of social and economic differences, especially for those who had little. Ideas on the improvement of society began to include the physical improvement of living conditions, not only in the housing, but in all aspects of life. Robert Owen's views have been mentioned previously in this direction. However, although housing was gradually dealt with and improved, progress was slow in dealing with the whole environment. Any changes which did take place were piecemeal, solutions for small areas rather than an overall advancement. Bournville and Port Sunlight were the attempts of benevolent industrialists to provide a total environment in which their employees could enjoy, not only high-quality accommodation, but also recreation, culture and a sense of community. All the ideas on economic and social progress were brought together by Ebenezer Howard (1850–1928) in 1898, when he published his pioneer book, *Tomorrow*.

Garden Cities and the neighbourhood

In his book, Howard produced a model for urban development which was to influence most of the designs of towns which followed, even to the present day. He proposed that urban areas should be clustered together, with small units related to a Central City. This large centre would provide a full range of services for the entire group, while the smaller units would be able to keep a sense of community. His organization tried to deal with the problem of the size of many urban growths, a size which tended to overpower the individual, and which has led to town-dwellers suffering more nervous illness than their country counterparts, brought about by loneliness and tension. Our "satellite towns" are a modern version of Howard's ideas.

Each of Howard's model towns was arranged around a

central core of public buildings, set within public parkland. The diagram in Figure 95 shows that this would be ringed by the shops which would serve the residential community. The housing itself was not planned at an exceptionally low density, about forty-two per hectare (seventeen per acre), but every house was to have its own garden. Within the housing area there was to be a ring of parkway, providing land for schools, churches and public open space. The perimeter would be for industrial use, which would be closely linked with the railway system. Communications played an important role in Howard's scheme, with radial boulevards thirty-six metres wide (120 feet) leading from the centre and connecting with concentric roads. The road layout was very advanced considering that the motor car was still an unusual occurrence in 1898.

The details of Howard's proposals were important, but of greater significance were the concepts on which they were based. Unlike earlier nineteenth-century British experiments in urban planning, Howard's scheme was not linked to any particular industries, and was intended as a model for all localities, drawn diagrammatically, but intended to be tailored to local conditions. It was a blueprint for a whole series of developments where the needs of the total community were to be considered and planned for. The small satellite towns were to be sub-divided into wards, each of about 5,000 people, within which there would be a suitable range of employment and services. Each ward was to include a mixture of social groups, avoiding the "ghetto" conditions which had arisen in the industrial towns. Community facilities, particularly schools, were to be centralized within the ward area. In Howard's scheme, planning had to deal with personal lives and not merely bricks and mortar.

Howard's ideas were partly incorporated into the building of Letchworth, the first Garden City, begun in 1903, in Hampstead Garden Suburb (1907) and Welwyn (1919). Hampstead was originally intended to be a mixture of all social groups and incomes living together, but, in fact, it remained dominantly middle-class. Its promoters had strong views on preserving the existing environment, as far as was possible, and in their literature stated: "We aim at preserving natural beauty. Our object is so to lay out the ground that every tree may be kept, hedgerows duly considered, and the foreground of the distant view be preserved. . . ." However, the new designs were best developed by the Americans who carried them a stage further. By 1920, they were using the term "Neighbourhood unit", associated chiefly with the work of the American Clarence Perry. He saw a healthy community as one which has a sensible assortment and location of all the community facilities. First among these he placed the elementary, or primary, school, which he considered should be at the centre of the area. As the children had to be able to walk to and from school the limits of the community were set at about one kilometre from the centre. This area

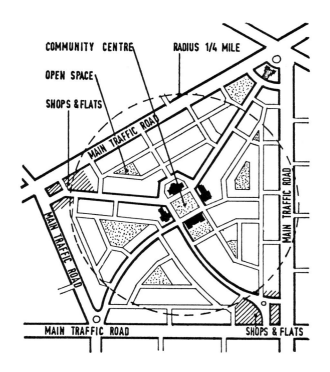

Above: Fig. 96 **Perry's Neighbourhood Unit.**

would contain a population of about 5,000. With this number, most people could be expected to know many of the others in the group. Community open space would be available. Arterial roads would carry heavy traffic outside the area; local traffic would have its own distributor roads. For the first time, it was suggested that pedestrians should be segregated from the traffic. It was, in many ways, inevitable that this thought should arise in the USA, where the large-scale ownership of vehicles was more advanced than in Europe.

In the 1920s, the idea of planning communities was extended by the development of the Radburn plan, so-called because the design was first put forward for the proposed new town of Radburn, New Jersey. It used the neighbourhood principle, basing its size on the intake, or catchment, of a centrally-placed primary school. With this would be an allied cultural centre and a recreation area. It was in Radburn that the segregation of pedestrians and vehicles was first put into practice. The houses were linked to *cul-de-sacs*, service roads at the rear of the houses, which fed into the main network. Pedestrians used paths, which began at the front of the houses, and were cut through traffic-free parkland. When they had to cross the road system, they did so by way of underpasses. Figure 97 shows

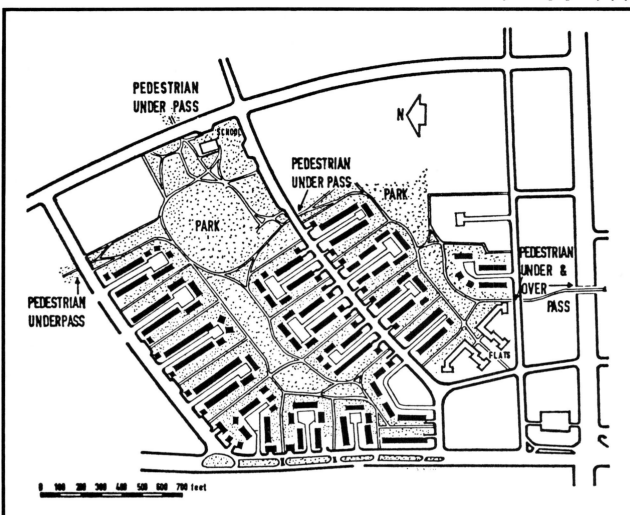

PEDESTRIAN
UNDER PASS

SCHOOL

PEDESTRIAN
UNDER PASS

PARK

N

PARK

PEDESTRIAN
UNDER &
OVER
PASS

PEDESTRIAN
UNDERPASS

FLATS

0 100 200 300 400 500 600 700 feet

Above: Fig. 97   **The arrangement of Radburn, New Jersey.**

Below: Fig. 98   **A street in Radburn planning.**

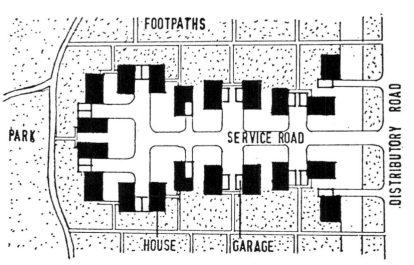

FOOTPATHS

PARK

SERVICE ROAD

DISTRIBUTORY ROAD

HOUSE   GARAGE

how this arrangement works. The ideas, originated in the USA, have had a great impact on the design of later British towns.

Meanwhile, in the twenties and thirties in Britain, the workings of the 1919 Town and Country Planning Act were taking effect. The estates which were built because of it were of much-reduced density, averaging 25–30 houses per hectare (10–12 per acre). Together with the speculative private estates which were built in great numbers in the 1930s, due to easier financing by building societies, the Act produced much of the suburbia which we see today. There was little in the way of control over the social environment, in most cases. Economic forces still dominated. Community life received little help and, if it grew at all, it was because of the enthusiasm and interest of the residents themselves. Many of the estates were social deserts and, in Britain, we continued with the same practice for many years. The major British contribution to town development during this period came with the ideas on precincts of Sir Alker Tripp (1883–1954), published in 1942. It was a British version of a Radburn organization, with the roads graded to carry traffic either through or within the area, and with shopping and community facilities accessible by footpaths. The precincts themselves were to be traffic-free, although they were only planned as small local features, not as the large, city-centre precincts we have today.

New Towns

The most important British advance of this century came after the Second World War with the New Town movement. During the war, a series of reports had been prepared, planning the direction Britain would take after war had finished. Some, like the Barlow and Beveridge Reports, dealt with aspects of social and economic planning and after the war their proposals were put into practice. The 1947 Town and Country Planning Act was the most far-reaching of all these Acts, in that it brought almost all building construction and development under national control, requiring planning permission. Regional plans were to be prepared for all parts of the country, National Parks were proposed and, in urban development, New Towns were to be built. "New" was a carefully chosen adjective; they were meant to be a break from the past, not just another formless expansion of the town into the countryside. All over Britain, a new period of urban growth was taking place, both in local authority and private estates. Much of it was going on to replace war-damaged dwellings. As these had usually been high-density terraces, re-housing at the lower densities led to an increase in the urban area. As well as this, new houses were needed to provide decent living standards for thousands whose houses had not been destroyed, but which were lacking in modern amenities, often classified as "unfit for human habitation", and needing to be demolished. In the same manner as in the 1920s and 1930s, new estates spread out.

The New Towns were thought of as the answer to many of the problems which were so obvious in the industrial slums and which had not been dealt with by other twentieth-century developments. Merely building houses and gardens, as in the suburban estates, was no answer to the difficulties. The New Towns used all the ideas which had developed from the nineteenth century onwards.

The importance of New Towns can be measured from the fact that when all those already designated have been built, about 3½ million people, over six per cent of the population of the United Kingdom, will live in them. Not all of them are really "New" – some are grafted onto existing urban areas, but they represent a very important feature of urban development, in that they are attempting to find answers for problems which we have been unable to solve over the last hundred and fifty years.

There are, of course, extensions of urban areas which do not have a guiding Master Plan as do the New Towns, but they do have some form of overall control. Now, we can see in our towns and cities a full spectrum of social attitude, beginning with the results of a relatively unplanned and profit-guided approach, which can give either architectural gems or slums, leading through to the New Towns. The final development is an attempt to marry together the community warmth of the slums with the benefits of better house design. The final section of this book deals with a real New Town, one which shows many of the features of organization and character which have been outlined so far, although it must be remembered that each New Town has its own special plan and set of attitudes.

It would be very simple if, as one moved outwards from the urban centre, each new development succeeded the previous one, so that there were progressively more modern features. However, most suburban areas are a hotch-potch of different styles, lay-outs and approaches. Because of the relatively recent introduction of planning controls, our suburbs contain exclusive mansions, local authority "high-rise", the remains of pre-industrial villages, mixed together with other varieties. The patterns in any particular district can partly be explained by progress in planning and design, but local factors often cause peculiar variations. The importance of social value has already been mentioned; there are also the relic effects of past land ownership, the presence of manorial estates which have been turned into parkland, and a multitude of other factors.

As in all aspects of urban study, there is no substitute for observation and investigation for solving problems. The information and attitudes contained in this book are only guidelines, to be tested and examined within the framework of real areas. There are so many ways to study a particular locality, that it is not possible to give an easy guide to the correct method. Besides this, every town has its own special dominating feature; in some, it may be medieval remains, in others twentieth-century modernistic, so that there is no single rigid approach.

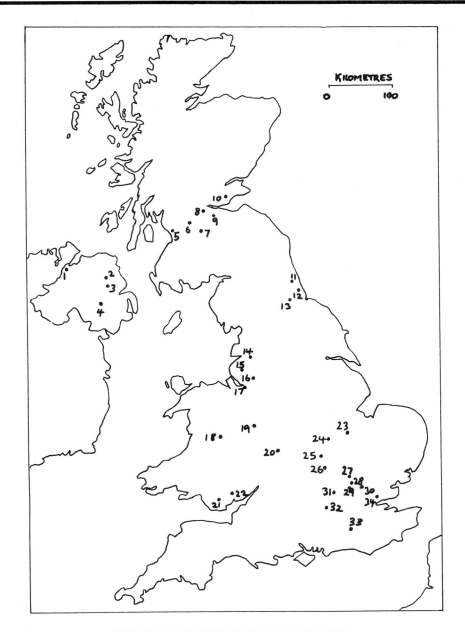

DESIGNATED NEW TOWNS IN THE UK

N. IRELAND
1. LONDONDERRY
2. BALLYMENA
3. ANTRIM
4. CRAIGAVON

SCOTLAND
5. IRVINE
6. E. KILBRIDE
7. STONEHOUSE
8. CUMBERNAULD
9. LIVINGSTON
10. GLENROTHES

NORTH-EAST ENGLAND
11. WASHINGTON
12. PETERLEE
13. AYCLIFFE

NORTH-WEST ENGLAND
14. CENTRAL LANCASHIRE
15. SKELMERSDALE
16. WARRINGTON
17. RUNCORN

WEST MIDLANDS/ MID WALES
18. NEWTOWN
19. TELFORD
20. REDDITCH

SOUTH WALES
21. LLANTRISANT
22. CWMBRAN

SOUTH-EAST ENGLAND
23. PETERBOROUGH

24. CORBY
25. NORTHAMPTON
26. MILTON KEYNES
26. STEVENAGE
28. WELWYN GARDEN CITY
29. HATFIELD
30. HARLOW
31. HEMEL HEMPSTEAD
32. BRACKNELL
33. CRAWLEY
34. BASILDON

Case study: Runcorn – old and new

Section I

Runcorn is situated on the left bank of the Mersey estuary. It has no particular claim to historical fame, although it was referred to as a settlement as early as AD 915. Before the eighteenth century, Runcorn is mentioned only as a minor port, subsidiary in importance to its present-day suburb of Halton, which had a prominent castle. Very little remains of the landscape built before 1750, and the critical date in the development of Runcorn as an urban area was 1773, when Runcorn locks were opened at the end of the Duke of Bridgewater's Canal. The canal was completed in 1776, connecting Manchester to the Mersey estuary and isolating part of the area in that, sandwiched between the line of the canal and the river, its direction of growth was controlled for almost a hundred years. It became known as the Island; canals, which caused its separation, were to be responsible for most of its urban growth over the following century.

The population of Runcorn rose rapidly from the period of the end of the eighteenth century; the statistics are shown in Figure 99. Eighteen hundred and four saw another canal connected to the estuary, this time the extension of the Mersey and Irwell Navigation. Canal traffic and the trans-shipment of goods led to a rapid rise in manufacturing. By 1811, out of 400 families registered in the Census, only 34 relied on agriculture for their living and 339 were involved in manufacturing. The industries operating at that time were mainly soap and acid works, along with a brewery, a skinyard (tannery) and a timber yard/smithy. There was still a windmill in operation and local sandstone was quarried and shipped out. Industrial growth brought more workers, and more houses. As in most of the growing industrial areas, they were courts and terraces, built in the streets whose names give an indication of their period of construction. Regent and Brunswick are followed by Peel and Wellington. At the same time, public buildings began to multiply: churches, chapels, schools and large numbers of public houses. Many of these are still part of the present landscape, very little altered in appearance.

Although the area grew quickly, there was still open space and greenery, even on the Island. As late as 1844 there was an orchard in the High Street, and visitors came to the town, drawn by its reputation as a health resort. Sea bathing in the Mersey was very popular, and led to the building of Seawater Baths in 1822. The area of the shore where the railway bridge now stands was described in these terms in

1834: "This is a very pleasant part of the shore, particularly when the tide is in. The high, green hedge affording protection from the rays of the sun behind, the rapid water flowing at our feet and the life and interest given to the scenery around by the various vessels passing before the eye, render it a delightful retreat, both for the resident, and for the visitor." The writer would have found it difficult to use these terms in later periods, when the Mersey, made up of sewage and chemical waste, became renowned for its filthy colour. Even at the time the passage was written the environment was not so attractive for the workers in the soaperies and tanneries. They lived in crowded, insanitary conditions. In 1832, cholera broke out and, between June and October, 36 cases were confirmed, of whom 18 died. Hurriedly, a Board of Health was formed to "adopt measures for the removal of nuisances". In fact, Runcorn was very advanced in dealing with its problems. It had the usual jumble of streets and courts, built without control, from a variety of materials, and the problems connected with high-density living, side by side with foul-smelling industries, forced the Parish Council into action. They were very strong on the removal of nuisances – dangerous and

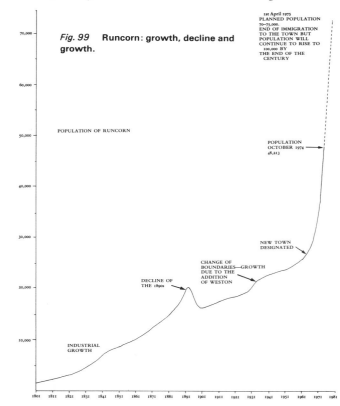

Fig. 99   Runcorn: growth, decline and growth.

Above: Fig. 100   Detail from map of Runcorn surveyed in 1832–33. Comment: Notice the back-to-backs on the left, and also the fact that there is still open space available.

insanitary houses, or cesspits which were not cleaned regularly. In earlier chapters, the dangers of fire in the medieval town were stressed, and they were still very much alive in the last century. As late as 1840, at a Runcorn Vestry Meeting, it was unanimously agreed that "whilst they would express their gratitude to that Allwise providence who has hitherto mercifully protected them from the calamities of fire, nevertheless deem it their imperative duty, in humble dependance upon the same providence for the protection of their lives and property against the perils of fire as providence dictates and as experience in other large and populous places has proved to be necessary. To that end, they recommend that a Fire Engine, or Engines, be provided." The language used is somewhat complicated, probably so that the "Allwise providence" would not be too offended because his care was not considered sufficient, but it is clear that the need to control the fortunes of the area was to have a backyard space of at least 180 square feet accepted, little was done, and no engines were actually bought.

There were no Acts in force to deal with the features of Runcorn's landscape in the 1840s, although part of the Lighting and Watching Act was adopted in 1836. This brought gas lamps to the main streets, with lamp-posts "of good, solid, English oak", 10 feet 6 inches (3·2 metres) high and 8 inches (20 centimetres) square. Otherwise, the pattern of the town developed along normal industrial lines with foundries, soaperies and other chemical works lining the banks of the canals, timber and boat yards along the river, and the churches, schools and houses crammed between them. The Bridgewater Canal acted as a natural barrier to development; any expansion took place between it and the river, moving east and west from the town nucleus. There was little besides a few isolated cottages between industrial Runcorn's growth, declined from the middle of the 1880s. Dominating the town and the area around were the chimneys of the soaperies and the tanneries, the tallest ones being over 90 metres (about 300 feet). The photograph in Figure 101 shows late nineteenth-century Runcorn, and it has all the flavour of any industrial settlement of the time.

Above: Fig. 101 **Nineteenth-century industrial Runcorn.**

The smoke, and more especially the smells, made it a low-income town; anyone with money lived on the hills of Halton or Higher Runcorn. The water supply, as in so many other places, was polluted by industry, and in the 1840s the Bridgewater Estate Trustees, who controlled most of the land use, were asked to deal with discharge from the soaperies, "which contaminates the water used by the public generally".

The Parish Council was never really strong enough to deal properly with all the problems and it became clear that some more powerful agent was needed to organize the district. In 1851, preliminary enquiries were made to apply to Parliament for permission to introduce an Improvement Bill. In 1852, the Runcorn Improvement Act was passed and the Improvement Commissioners became the chief power in Runcorn. From then, until Runcorn gained urban status in the 1890s, the Commissioners altered the landscape by passing a series of bye-laws which controlled many of the features of the buildings and streets. Many of the bye-laws were in advance of their time. For example, by 1860, cellar dwellings were banned and every dwelling of two storeys was to have a backyard space of at least 180 square feet (16·7 square metres). Every habitable room was to have at least one window, and the total area of windows in each room was to be at least 12 square feet (0·9 square metres). Also they had to be capable of opening; another victory for Victorian ventilation. We may not think the standards very high, but they compared well with many other towns. The

houses shown in Figure 103 date from the time of the Improvement Commissioners, who used the penalties of the 1848 Public Health Act to reinforce their early work and adapted their standards to later Acts. The scene shown in the photograph is of housing built in the 1850s and 1860s. The quality was high enough to last for a hundred years, and in some cases to allow modernization for a future generation.

While the town was growing, the beginning of its decline was becoming apparent. From 1831 the profits of the Bridgewater Canal Company fell because of competition from the Liverpool and Manchester Railway. By 1850, new industrial development slowed, particularly because the Bridgewater Trustees, who controlled property in Runcorn with a rateable value of two-thirds of the town's total, discouraged new chemical works. Instead, they opened across the river at Widnes. The railways took away more and more of the canal trade and the docks, the cause of Runcorn's growth, declined from the middle of the 1880s. The decline was made more pronounced when, in spite of Runcorn's opposition, the Manchester Ship Canal was constructed, eventually opening in 1894. This cut off Runcorn from the open sea and killed the shipyards. Large vessels, up to 12,000 tons (12,192 tonnes), used the Ship Canal, and they called infrequently at Runcorn. The Bridgewater Canal traffic fell away, and by the beginning of the First World War, there were only 44 canal boats registered at Runcorn, compared with 116 twenty years previously. The railway came to Runcorn but brought little

Above: Fig. 102 **The Bridgewater as a working canal.**

Right: Fig. 103 **The landscape of the Improvement Commissioners.**

benefit, and a major intrusion into the landscape. A massive viaduct (Figure 106) cut through the area and beneath it the terraces appeared as dolls' houses.

The effects of economic decline were long-lasting, and explain much of the landscape today. In what is now called the Old Town, that is mainly the section between the Bridgewater and Ship Canals, the slowing-down of economic growth led to a halt in new building. Very few of the older buildings were replaced, because of reduced demand. Between 1891 and 1901 the population declined by twenty per cent, and, in 1901, 532 houses out of a total of 3,434 were unoccupied. In terms of demand for land, and bid rents, the Runcorn of this period had few attractive features. Wages were low, overcrowding was common, and little new housing appeared. There had been a spilling-over of the town across the Bridgewater Canal, but the advance was stopped by economic conditions. The shops which had developed along High Street, Church Street and Bridge Street suffered and the new public buildings of the time often came from benefactors, rather than from the rates. Sir John Brunner (1842–1919), the chemical magnate, one of the founders of the companies which were to become ICI, gave the Guildhall, and the Library was built, like so many in Britain, from funds provided by Andrew Carnegie.

Above: Fig. 104 Runcorn in 1875. Notice the industries of the riverside and the seawater baths. The Island area changes very little after this time.

Below: Fig. 105 Runcorn in 1912. The Ship Canal controls the waterfront.

As the buildings and the streets remained unchanged, so did the conditions of the people within them. In 1885, the Improvement Commissioners were still dealing with matters such as the removal of sewage and, in that year, agreed, "That the advertisement inviting tenders for the removal of night soil be inserted in the *Liverpool Mercury*, *Runcorn Guardian* and the *Runcorn Examiner*." In 1892, the Medical Officer of Health, in his annual report, commented on the conditions in the town and their effects. He stated

"I may mention here that there was some strong suspicion held in some quarters that when 2 or 3 cases of fever were notified from one house, they might be typhus fever, as it was held to be rather unusual to find enteric

fever attacking the household by turns. I regret to say that in some parts of the town, where fever was most prevalent, many houses were not free of the evils of overcrowding, and in these cases, there was a persistent disposition on the part of the householder [*i.e.* the landlord] to conceal these conditions from the authorities."

and

"In reporting to the Authority so recently on the prevalence of typhoid fever, I took occasion then to state what seemed to be the chief factor in propagating this insidious form of disease. I am also aware that the Authority are doing all in their power to remedy an evil which has been growing for so many years. The faulty construction of ash pits and privy pits, and the generally sewage soaked condition of the soil has to a large extent to account, in my opinion, for the recurrence of this disease."

In spite of all the Public Health and Housing Acts passed through Parliament, parts of Runcorn entered the twentieth century in this state.

Below: Fig. 106 **Under the shadow of the railway. A massive viaduct links Runcorn and Widnes. Some idea of its size can be gained from the fact that the arches in the background are of the same bridge as in the foreground. They dwarf the terraces; notice Brindley Street, named after the engineer responsible for the building of the Bridgewater, James Brindley (1716–72).**

Section 2

Changes did take place in Runcorn during the first half of the twentieth century, but they were perhaps more limited than in most British urban areas. As in most areas there was a physical expansion of the town, due, not to more people, but to a slow improvement in the quality of the environment. The first real slum clearance came in 1913, when a new school playground was created by the demolition of some back-to-backs. Addison's Act of 1919 prompted the Urban District Council (created in 1894) to propose two Council estate areas, outside the margins of the existing urban area. These, completed in 1922, added a hundred houses to the stock of the town. More importantly, they began the rapid expansion in area which marked the 1920s and 1930s. From the Old Town, settlement spread up the hills towards Upper Runcorn and Halton. Most of the developments were private, aided by the availability of cheap mortgages which allowed people to buy their own homes, but the Council was also active, having built over three hundred houses by 1938. The density of these new districts varied, but they were seldom more than thirty per hectare, with the private housing being at twenty to twenty-five. The effect of low-density growth was to double the built-up area of the town within twenty years, although its population only grew because of boundary changes in 1936. This brought in the suburban district of Weston, as well as the ICI chemical works situated there.

Although there was this expansion, the Old Town remained the focus of the community. Services were still centred there, and with them the administrative, commercial and social life of the town. In common with

Above: Fig. 107 The end of the canal. The photograph is taken from the in-filled section of one of the Bridgewater locks. There is a basin to the right, used for off-loading. The gate paddles and dock mechanism is still present. Over the canal is the Waterloo bridge built 1830–31.

most estate development, few shops were built in the new areas and the same was true of other social facilities. The Old Town had a concentration of public houses, the traditional meeting-point of social life, with the majority of them being situated on the terraced-street corners, although there were a number of higher-class "hotels", where the more sophisticated could meet. There was also a cinema, a theatre, numerous clubs and associations, and the church halls. Commercially, almost all the professional services and offices were in the Island area, except for those connected with ICI. Most of the premises were small; both shops and offices were limited in their growth by the general lack of prosperity in the town. The corner shop was still the commonest form of shop organization, although, in the centre, there were a small number of regional and national chain stores such as Boots the Chemist. There was one notable exception to the concentration of facilities. The Town Hall had changed its location from the nineteenth-century centre, out to suburbia. In 1933, the centre of administration moved to a chemical manufacturer's mansion of the 1850s. This move might be taken as a comment on the restrictions imposed by cramped town-centre conditions, or as a wish to be more associated with the pleasanter areas of the town.

Above: Fig. 108 Industrial stagnation. This part of the canal was important for smelting and ship-building one hundred years ago. Now it has no industrial use, the buildings of the Bridgewater Foundry – to the right – are used by scrap-metal dealers.

If very little seemed to change in Runcorn, it was because of its limited economic development. Towns develop and change mainly in relation to the pace of economic growth. Runcorn began the century with problems which stemmed from its reliance on industries whose fortunes were under some form of cloud. The range of these industries had shrunk to chemicals, leather, stone, ironfounding, dock and canal traffic and small-boat repair. None of these, with the exception of the ICI works at Weston, were to remain major employers up till the present. The soap, acid and alkali works closed down during the 1930s, being old and uneconomic. Tanning had a period of prosperity, reaching a peak during the 1930s, when it employed 1,100 people, over ten per cent of the employed population. However, it declined in the face of foreign competition. The introduction of synthetic shoe soles in the late 1950s finally killed it off, and the tanneries all closed during the 1960s. The foundries changed their use, or fell into disrepair, and the shipyards declined, until now all that is left is work for the Ship Canal Company. Traffic on the Bridgewater fell away so much that the Bridgewater lock into the Ship Canal, and the "Duke's Steps" leading down to it, became disused from 1953. The section from Waterloo Bridge was eventually in-filled. The industrial decline was progressive and little came to replace the derelict industries. Fortunately, the chemical centres of Weston and Widnes provided some local employment; otherwise it was necessary to travel outside the area. The effect of this was to limit the development of Runcorn so that it did little more than replace itself, at a slow rate. Population rose hardly at all; no new centres grew up, and the old areas remained as they were.

If this had continued, then Runcorn today would be like several of the industrial settlements which rose up in the last century. Tucked away in isolated parts of Lancashire, Yorkshire and the North Midlands, they grew quickly, and, when they became redundant, they stagnated and died. By the beginning of the Second World War Runcorn had many of the features of such settlements. High-density living, little open space, limited social and recreational facilities, these were the main characteristics, made worse by being surrounded by decaying industrial sites. Outside the centre were estates of the recent past, provided with gardens but lacking community features, with the exception of schools, a few convenience shops and scattered churches. The growth of these estates was limited because if they did expand, they became even more isolated from the town-centre facilities.

The town today is very different; it attracts visitors from all over the world to see its special features. The conversion has taken place since the Second World War, and it has involved changes in organization, some of which are already present in a few of our urban areas, and others which Runcorn is pioneering.

Section 3

After the Second World War, the pace of change began to increase. The end result of it has been the transformation of the area because of its New Town status. Although Runcorn was not designated as a New Town until 1964, there was a build-up of planning towards the event, so that many things which happened before that date can only be explained by later factors. For example, one of the most important dates in Runcorn's history was 1961, when a road bridge across the Mersey was opened. However, the forward planning for this produced changes many years before. The approach roads for the bridge were cut through the mid nineteenth-century terraces and, thirteen years before the opening of the new link, the first steps were taken to rehouse the people who would become homeless because of clearance. The bridge itself became a symbol of the new Runcorn, and its construction was a reflection of, and a reason for, other changes.

In 1905, Runcorn was linked to Widnes by a transporter bridge, which, for the first time, allowed vehicles to cross the river at this point. The transporter was a platform hung from a girder framework which spanned the river. It was pulled backwards and forwards across the gap, with passengers and vehicles on it. However, it could carry few vehicles at one time, was stopped by strong winds and there were ever-increasing traffic jams of vehicles waiting to cross. In reality, Runcorn was cut off from the north bank of the estuary in terms of modern transport standards, and its links in other directions were none too good either. The new bridge was the first step in plans to change this situation. It was necessary because New Towns are not accidental creations, and they are not economic fairy-lands, where people live in attractive surroundings with nothing to do but admire their environment. Like any other urban area, New Towns rely on some form of industry to employ the population. If they fail to attract firms and businesses, they decline. The road bridge, and the linkage in the 1970s to the nearby motorway M56, provided access to good fast communications. Only with this change could expansion take place.

The New Town was announced in 1964, and two years later the Master Plan was produced. Here were outlined the concepts on which were based the growth from a population of under 30,000 to one of 100,000. A New Town Plan is a document which looks at the whole development, not just sections of it. It deals with industry, housing, transport, shopping and recreation, and hopes to find answers to the problems of urban life which have become obvious elsewhere. Every New Town has its own particular contribution and that of Runcorn is probably its transport system.

Dealing with the problems caused by the increasing demands of the car has become one of the major difficulties within our existing urban areas. Car owners want speedy mobility, with well-connected road networks. They want through-routes with few intersections or pedestrian crossings, and would like parking space to be available at all points. But cars are used mainly at peak hours, when people are travelling to and from work. Roads built to cope with these peaks would remain under-used for much of the day. Making private transport very efficient often means that public transport suffers by comparison. Fewer people than expected travel on buses and it often becomes uneconomic to operate frequent services. People without cars are isolated while much of the urban area is taken up with highways and car parks, using space which could have been used for recreation and open space. Runcorn hopes to find a balance between the private car and public transport. The new communities within the town are arranged on either side of a main public transport route, and the greatest distance from the houses to the road is less than five hundred metres. This distance, equal to a walking time of five minutes, is supposed to be the maximum car owners will walk before they decide to take the car instead. When they arrive at the road, they find Runcorn's chief transport innovation. The public transport route is the Busway, a road reserved for high-speed buses, which travel around their own system at an average speed of over 32 kmph (about 20 mph) including the time spent picking up passengers. Between stops they can travel at over 60 kmph. Their high speed is due to their not having to fight for space with other road users; there are no traffic jams to slow them down and their maintenance costs are less because they are not continually stopping and starting. Together with the Busway is an arrangement of expressways which provide a normal road network of motorway standard. These are situated outside the residential area and linked to them by local, distributor roads, as shown in Figures 111 and 112.

The idea of five minutes walking time also controls the distribution of local shopping and community facilities. These are planned to be along the Busway at about 0·8 kilometre (half-mile) intervals; Figure 109 shows the arrangement of them in the Master Plan, with the road system organized in a "figure of eight" pattern. Each of the local centres serves about 8,000 people within a radius of around 460 metres (500 yards), or, again, an average of five minutes walking time. The population figure corresponds to the one previously used in the idea of neighbourhood units, and Runcorn districts are organized on this basis. Each community of 8,000 is sub-divided into smaller neighbourhoods of approximately 2,000, and these are further split into residential groups of 100–200 persons. Each community has its own primary school, or schools, as in the American model. These are based around the local shopping centre, with four forms of primary intake for each community.

If 8,000 people have to live, at most, 0·8 km. from the local centre, then their average density would be 125 persons per hectare. Government housing directions suggest that, for every 1,000 people, there should be 10 hectares of

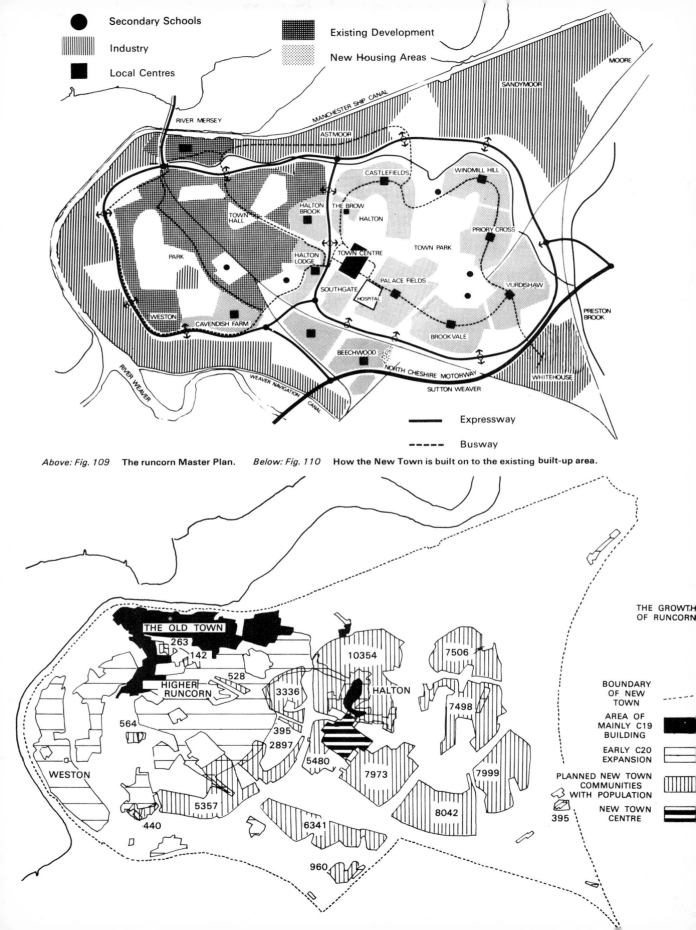

Legend (top)

- ● Secondary Schools
- ▥ Industry
- ■ Local Centres
- ▦ Existing Development
- ▒ New Housing Areas

Map labels (Fig. 109)

MOORE · SANDYMOOR · MANCHESTER SHIP CANAL · RIVER MERSEY · ASTMOOR · CASTLEFIELDS · WINDMILL HILL · TOWN HALL · HALTON BROOK · THE BROW · HALTON · PRIORY CROSS · PARK · HALTON LODGE · TOWN CENTRE · TOWN PARK · MURDISHAW · PALACE FIELDS · PRESTON BROOK · WESTON · SOUTHGATE · HOSPITAL · CAVENDISH FARM · BROOKVALE · BEECHWOOD · WHITEHOUSE · NORTH CHESHIRE MOTORWAY · SUTTON WEAVER · RIVER WEAVER · WEAVER NAVIGATION CANAL

—— Expressway

- - - - - Busway

Above: Fig. 109 **The runcorn Master Plan.** *Below: Fig. 110* **How the New Town is built on to the existing built-up area.**

Map labels (Fig. 110)

THE OLD TOWN · 263 · 142 · 528 · 10354 · 7506 · HIGHER RUNCORN · 3336 · HALTON · 7498 · 564 · 395 · 5480 · 7973 · 7999 · WESTON · 2897 · 5357 · 7973 · 8042 · 440 · 6341 · 960

THE GROWTH OF RUNCORN

- BOUNDARY OF NEW TOWN
- ■ AREA OF MAINLY C19 BUILDING
- ▤ EARLY C20 EXPANSION
- ▥ PLANNED NEW TOWN COMMUNITIES WITH POPULATION
- ◇
- ■ NEW TOWN CENTRE
- 395

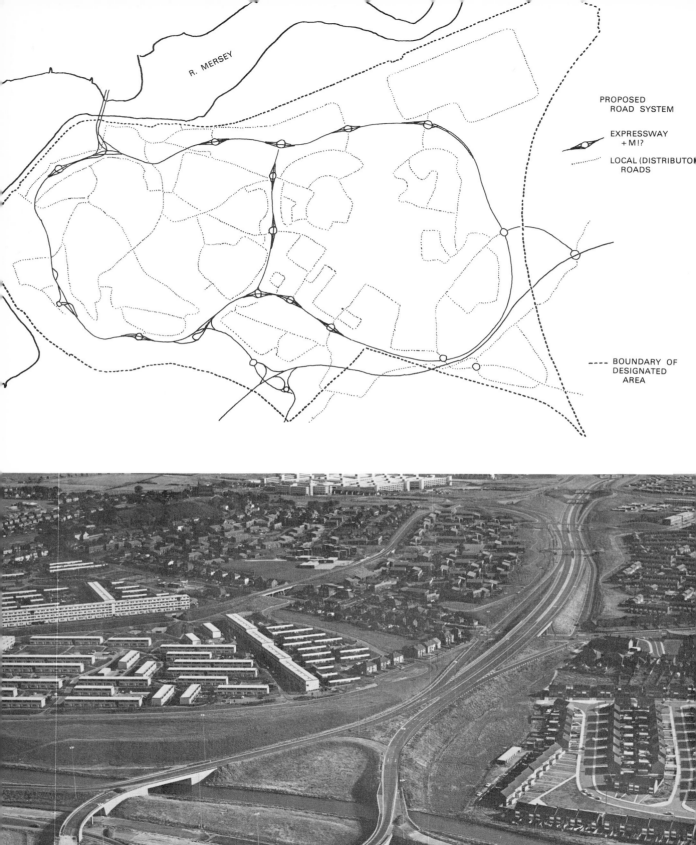

PROPOSED
ROAD SYSTEM

EXPRESSWAY
+ M !?

LOCAL (DISTRIBUTOR
ROADS

BOUNDARY OF
DESIGNATED
AREA

R. MERSEY

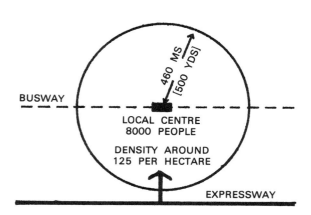

Above: Fig. 114   **Award-winning estate development. Palace Fields, Runcorn.** *Below: Fig. 115*

Opposite page: top: Fig. 111   **The proposed road system.**
Opposite page: bottom: Fig. 112   **The expressways. This shows the central spine of the "figure of eight". The section in the foreground is not yet complete, but the ease of movement can be appreciated. Each of the estates in the picture is of a different plan, so that there is no monotony of landscape.**

Above: Fig. 113   **Local centres related to walking distance.**

space allowed for schools, roads and shops. Taking this amount away from the area of the community means that the density is, in fact, over 150 people per hectare. This would be over 40 houses per hectare, considerably more than were used in the estates of fifty years ago. Higher densities than this will be found near the district centres, as Figure 115 shows. The justification for these densities comes because of the land released for recreational open space. Nearly thirty per cent of the area of the New Town will be in open space. Playing fields are planned to cover 190 hectares, woodland 226 hectares, and, in the central part of the newly developed section, there is the extensive Town Park around which are built the new neighbourhood communities. The houses themselves, although high-density, are to be surrounded by landscaped gardens, giving an impression of a semi-rural situation and increasing the sense of privacy. Figure 114 shows an example of this type of landscape. The groups of houses are arranged on the principle of Radburn planning, facing onto walkways at the front, with groups of garages in the *cul-de-sacs* in the rear.

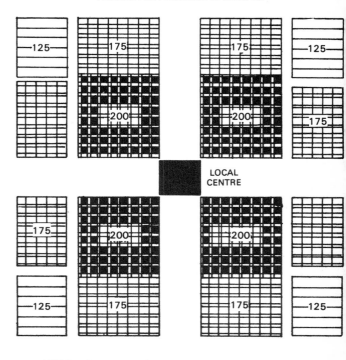

DENSITY OF PEOPLE WITHIN THE COMMUNITY

FIGURES ARE PERSONS PER HECTARE

NOTICE HOW DENSITIES ARE INCREASED NEAR TO THE CENTRE

As well as having shopping facilities, the district centres are community developments. The schools are planned to be used for cultural and recreational matters in out-of-school hours and each 8,000 community will have a clinic, dental and medical centres, as well as three public houses. In the Master Plan, the centres are put forward as "places where people can have a cup of coffee and a chat as well as do their shopping". However, the major focus of social life will be the Town Centre. The old centre, in the Old Town, has been replaced by one situated at the centre of the "figure of eight" transport system. There is space for four blocks of development in the centre, and the first to be completed is the spectacular Shopping City, shown in Figure 116. This is as great a contrast with the facilities within the Old Town as is possible to imagine. The building cost £10 million by the time it was completed in 1971. Faced in white tiles, it provides an air-conditioned precinct, with over 100 shops, along with banks and snack bars. There is parking space for 2,400 cars on the lower floors. From the Busway stop, escalators lead up to the shops or down to a regional and national bus station. The Shopping City is the first of the planned units and it has already been joined by an office block with local and national administration centred within it. The Centre will eventually grow into a full range of commercial, cultural and entertainment facilities. The first part of a large central hospital complex has been built and there are plans for a central library and a College of Further Education. It will make a highly-centralized town, but, in this case, it can be justified because of the easy communications between the Centre and the outlying districts.

All these details and plans would be irrelevant if there were no employment for the population. In earlier sections it could be seen that the industry which existed before the New Town was hardly very dynamic. The 1960s had seen the final death throes of the tanneries and ICI remained as the only large employer of labour. Even they could not be relied on to expand fast enough to take up the increased population. It was possible for people to live in Runcorn

Below: Fig. 116 **Shopping city and Halton Castle. The modern blocks of Shopping City contrast with the medieval settlement of Halton, still with the remnants of a more recent castle.**

New Town and to work in Widnes or south Liverpool, but it was obviously more convenient if they could work near to their homes. In 1966, Runcorn was granted Development Area status, which meant that Government grants were available to tempt new industry to the town. There were certain advantages which would attract new firms. The road communications were the main asset, with the town expressways linked to the national motorways. To the east is the M56 to Manchestr, the M6 and London. By 1977, the trans-Mersey road bridge will be increased to four-lane width, which will ease the traffic flow to Liverpool and to the M62, the Liverpool–Hull motorway. The building of the road bridge has had a great effect on the stagnant traffic of Runcorn docks. In the last ten or fifteen years the amount of freight handled has increased by ten times. Runcorn is even favoured by new rail developments; the electrified London–Liverpool line allows businessmen to be in London in just over two hours.

Besides these advantages, there was the availability of labour and land. The former came from the increasing population; the latter from the Development Corporation. Whereas the industry in old Runcorn had surrounded and dominated the town, the new industries were allocated estates on the perimeter. There, linked closely to the expressways and the Busway, raw materials, workers and finished products could be easily shifted. The industrial types were very different from the acid works and soaperies which had such an adverse impact on the nineteenth-century landscape. Firstly, they were housed in single-storey units, large and modern with bright, clean working conditions. Secondly, they dealt with modern products. The most important newcomers have been breweries, giant plants for Guinness and Bass Charrington. Although they are chemical factories in their own way, they do not give out the dangerous fumes and effluent of their nineteenth-century predecessors. Runcorn also has England's first Japanese-owned factory, YKK zip fasteners, which came complete with Japanese executives.

Below: Fig. 117 **Runcorn Old and New. In the foreground the new town, in the rear the old. Note the contrasts in density which are evident between them.**

Section 4

The New Town is attractive. Even though the housing is medium-density, it is surrounded by gardens, and its paths are secluded and traffic-free. The service on the Busway is fast and frequent, buses arriving virtually every five minutes. Passengers are pleased with it, and bus drivers like it so much that they regret going back to the normal road system. The Shopping City has no difficulty in letting its shops, although new hypermarkets in the region around Runcorn are providing stiff competition. When Shopping City first opened people travelled 15 or 20 kilometres to visit it, but its future role is more likely to be as a supplier to the growing population of the New Town. The industrial estates have attracted a wide range of new industries and the community centres are used for an increasing variety of activities. One of the schools has had a bar fitted so that adults may use the building in the evening. Demand for the housing has been so great that the Development Corporation has stopped recruiting new settlers from Liverpool, its main source. Several of the buildings, including factories and houses, have won architectural awards, and every week there is a delegation from a foreign country, wishing to see the New Town and assessing its relevance to their own urban development. In 1975, 570 official visitors from 38 overseas countries came to the Development Corporation.

However, to pretend that everything is wonderful or perfect would be misleading. There are problems which New Town status has not solved, and may never do. Although social workers meet new settlers, and help them to fit into their new surroundings, there have been criticisms of the facilities. It may be, of course, that the new systems do not immediately compensate for the social attractions of the terraces from which most of the inhabitants have come. Whatever the reasons, the New Town is growing and changing, and should be able to come to terms with the new problems. It may be a generation before people feel at home in the different environment. However, it could be argued that the main difficulties are not with the new part of the New Town, but with the old part of the Old.

A century of neglect has made the Island physically unattractive. Until the New Town began, and the new shops, housing and industries grew, it had, at least, the advantages of being the central focus of the settlement. When the Shopping City opened as the nucleus of the new Town Centre, it speeded up the process of decline. Already, between 1951 and 1961, the population of the two central wards, Mersey and Bridgewater, had sharply declined because of slum clearance by the Council. Part of this was related to the line of the road bridge, which gave very little direct benefit to the Island area. Some small improvements took place, such as a new shopping area in Church Street, shown in Figure 120, and a market hall and bus station, built in 1961. However, the Old Town centre had no defences against the impact of New Town status. The most

Above: Fig. 118 **One example of many.**

Right above: Fig. 119 **Messages from a clearance area.** *Right below: Fig. 120* **Church Street Shopping Area. Half the shops are vacant, waiting for tenants who may never come.**

important blow came in respect of shopping, where many of the main stores in the old centre opened new, larger branches in Shopping City. Trade flowed to the new development, and gradually, more and more of the shops in the Island section closed down. At the end of 1974, out of 174 shops in the old centre, 60 were vacant, thirty-four per cent of the total. The photograph of the Church Street area shows that it was often the new buildings which suffered most, although the greatest desolation is along Bridge Street, where much of the housing has become derelict and the customers have departed. Besides the shops, other facilities were moved. The notice on the police station is typical of many of the Old Town.

Neglect was inevitable as shops closed and houses remained derelict. It was in many ways understandable that the difficulties should be blamed on the New Town development. There was still a strong sense of community in the Island, and people banded together to protest against what they considered to be victimization by the authorities. The Development Corporation was singled out, and especially the General Manager, Mr D. F. Banwell, who is obviously not the most popular person in the area shown in Figure 119. At the beginning of 1975 there was a rash of stickers in the shop windows of the Old Town, each saying: "THIS IS THE HEART OF RUNCORN. DON'T BREAK IT". It seems a

forlorn plea, for commercially the existing area has shrunk to a fraction of its former importance. The people in the suburban estates who used to come to Church Street and Bridge Street, go instead to Shopping City. Around the shopping area of the old centre, there are many rows of empty terraces, waiting for the bulldozer, and, where they have been cleared, the land often lies unused.

It was accepted in the Master Plan, that the Old Town would experience problems readjusting to the new situation. It began to seem as though the pace of change, and the scale of the problems, was greater than had been expected. So, in 1971, the first Amendment to the New Town Plan was published, making changes in the urban renewal planned for the older areas. The new programme hoped to produce "a pleasing environment, good communications and a thriving district centre". It seems unlikely that the Old Town centre can be changed quickly enough to compare in any way with the new developments. Its problems are those of any of the nineteenth-century urban areas, and it is probably unfair to suggest that New Town status has made them much worse. The changes which have taken place are part of a normal process, whereby towns and cities develop new features and a new landscape. In the case of Runcorn, a period of stagnation caused old features to remain, long after they might have been cleared and replaced. Then there was a time of rapid conversion with the New Town, so that it is possible to see the whole sequence of recent landscape, from early industrial to futuristic.

More changes took place in 1976, with the adoption of Amendment number two. Planning in a New Town is not a static process, whereby the original ideas are carried through irrespective of alterations in the area's circumstances. The new Amendment is concerned with providing more land for housing within the Designated Area of the New Town. An increase in the number of houses is necessary for three main reasons, two of which relate back to themes raised in other parts of this book. The Government has reduced the density of housing in the New Town, so that more land is required to build the stated number of dwellings. This number has changed as well in that, when the Master Plan was drawn up, it was based on the assumption that the average home would contain 3·5 people. In reality, the declining birth rate of the last ten years had meant a rapid decrease in family size, so that the figure per house in Runcorn is now only 3·1. The New Town has quite precise population targets so there will be more families than expected, therefore more houses needed. Finally, while the population will grow by immigration to between 70–75,000 by 1979 (it was 54,000 in April 1976), the second generation of New Town inhabitants should take the population to 100,000 by the end of the century. New housing will be required for these children now growing up in Runcorn. The Amendment which changed the land-use pattern of the Master Plan was not universally welcomed. The inhabitants of Moore, Daresbury and Preston Brook, settlements on the edge of the proposed new housing area, objected to the Amendment, and forced a public enquiry, which is an increasingly common way of dealing with disputes over planning. The Development Corporation won its case, but the point is an illustration of the difficulties involved in planning, when there are often major problems impeding a solution satisfactory to all parties.

Every urban area has its own characteristics, its own special features, but at the same time there are common elements. Some of the details of Runcorn's pattern will be duplicated in most towns and cities. It is these similarities of functional arrangement and of buildings, and the growth of controls and planning which produced them, which gives that touch of individuality which produces all the rich variety of urban areas.

Guide to further study

A study of a particular locality such as Runcorn must use the full range of approaches referred to in the appendices in this book. However, such a piece of work in a town of any size could take years of research and is outside the scope and interest of the general reader. For most the choice is between the outline study, as in the case of Runcorn, or more likely the detailed examination of a small area, a parish or a district. For the former there will be official records, maps, Census returns, previously-published local histories, council minutes and town plans. A useful guide to sources, which is itself valuable in providing dates for markets, fairs, transport developments, law and order improvement, and many other features, is

> J. Richardson, *Local Historian's Encyclopedia* (Historical Publications Ltd, 1974)

For the small-area large scale survey material increasingly comes from first hand or primary sources. The amount of documented material on urban districts is often small, especially in the case of fairly anonymous residential areas. Careful study of maps (large scale) and parish registers is useful but many characteristics are only available by direct observation. This book is primarily concerned with this approach. Its aim has been to encourage the study of the small components of the urban landscape rather than the broad outlines. Much of the information has been concerned with processes, sometimes acting on a national scale, but the intention has been that, when the processes are understood, the reader will be able to make sense of his or her surroundings by recognizing how general trends have produced particular results in individual urban landscapes.

Index

COMHAIRLE CHONTAE THÁ CLIATH

SC

Iter
a